Oth
by Melis

ADVENTURES IN WRITING (SERIES)

- 101 Creative Writing Exercises
- 10 Core Practices for Better Writing
- 1200 Creative Writing Prompts

Get all three books in one volume: *Adventures in Writing: The Complete Collection.*

NOVELS

- Engineered Underground (Metamorphosis Book One)

Melissa also writes children's books under the pen name Emmy Donovan

The Storyteller's Toolbox

What's the Story?
Building Blocks for Fiction Writing

Melissa Donovan

Swan Hatch Press | San Francisco

THE STORYTELLER'S TOOLBOX
What's the Story? Building Blocks for Fiction Writing

Copyright © 2016 by Melissa Donovan

First Edition, 2016
Published by Swan Hatch Press • Melissa Donovan

ISBN: 0997671300
ISBN 13: 9780997671308
Library of Congress Control Number: 2016910444

The Storyteller's Toolbox
What's the Story?
Building Blocks for Fiction Writing

Table of Contents

Introduction: What to Expect from This Book

What's a story? Is it character? Plot? Conflict? Change? Why do some stories fall flat with audiences while others sweep the globe, captivating people in every corner of the world?

Stories entertain us, taking our minds off the rigors of daily life. But stories do more than entertain. They comfort us with warmth and joy; they frighten us with horror and terror; they woo us with romance and dazzle us with adventure. They make us laugh when we're sad or make us cry when we're happy. Whether true or made-up, stories help us feel connected to our fellow humans. They keep us company when we're lonely. They foster empathy by showing us what it's like to walk in someone else's shoes. They challenge our worldviews with fresh perspectives that force us to think in new ways.

We use storytelling, both as writers and as readers, to understand ourselves, one another, and the world we live in. And rarely do we acknowledge the power that stories hold over us. Stories can change people and cultures—and even the world.

The television series *Star Trek* gave us legions of scientists and engineers. George Orwell's novel *1984* warned us that governments would use technology to rob civilians of their privacy—an omen that many fear has already come true.

To Kill a Mockingbird shined a light on cultural and systemic racial injustice and inspired activists to fight for equality. These are just a few examples of stories that literally changed the course of human history.

But stories are also personal. When we read a story about a hero who finds strength and resilience within, we feel stronger. Stories about good triumphing over evil give us hope. Stories about people overcoming struggles or finding ways to make their dreams come true inspire and motivate us.

We love stories. We celebrate stories. We need stories.

People will stay up all night reading a page-turner. They'll neglect their responsibilities to marathon-watch a television series. They will stand in line—they will even sleep on the street—to see their favorite movies. Entire subcultures have been built around stories—just ask the fans who attend Comic-Con every year, fans who shell out hundreds (if not thousands) of dollars to gather with fellow story lovers and honor their favorite films, television shows, books, video games, and comics, many of them costumed as their favorite characters. That's dedication to story, and it's a testament to the power of storytelling.

What to Expect from This Book

The luckiest among us are born storytellers with a gift for narrative. If you've ever seen someone silence a room, captivating every ear with a mesmerizing story, then you've experienced the power that a naturally talented storyteller possesses. But many of us need to work at the craft and develop our storytelling skills. We might have a knack for creating sympathetic characters, but we struggle to construct a compelling plot. Maybe we have dozens of notebooks filled with exciting story ideas, but hammering them into a cohesive narrative is a challenge. Perhaps we're gifted at crafting prose but need to work harder at designing settings or developing themes. Even the most talented writers find some areas of storytelling more difficult than others.

Writing stories comes easily to the lucky few, but for most of us, it's hard work that requires an elaborate set of skills. After all, stories are comprised of many moving parts: characters, plots, settings, and themes are the core elements of stories. But there's a lot more that goes into good storytelling: dialogue, action, description, and exposition, as well as a host of literary devices and storytelling techniques. Not to mention structure, point of view, tense, and voice. Understanding each of these elements and how they function together within a story empowers us to be better storytellers.

To master these building blocks of stories, we need to develop a vocabulary and aptitude for the many components that comprise stories.

When I first got serious about writing fiction, I searched bookstores for a basic book on storytelling. I wanted a simple primer that would help me learn and master the various components of a story, especially terms I needed to know as a storyteller. I'd hear authors talk about things like *deus ex machina* or the *turning point at the end of act one*. One expert would say, "Story is conflict." Another would say, "Story is character." Every time I thought I had a handle on all the elements of storytelling, I'd come across some new term that I'd never heard before, or I'd be reminded of a concept that I'd forgotten about.

I found plenty of books on character creation or plot

development and even more on structure and formulas. There were lots of books on writing in genre. I even found some that promised to show me how to write a story—step-by-step instructions for producing a novel. But I never did find a book that simply gathered all the elements of storytelling in one place, a book that said, "Here are your tools and materials. Now go build something."

After years of studying stories, writing stories, coaching fellow storytellers, and editing a range of written works, I finally decided to write that book—a primer for fiction writers who want to master the building blocks of storytelling.

This book is designed to provide you with a basic but comprehensive understanding of those building blocks—the elements that work together to form a story. Using a range of stories* from books, films, and television shows as examples, we'll examine the components of good storytelling and explore how they fit together.

My hope is that you'll come away with a broader understanding of stories, what they are made of, and how they are developed. And I hope you gain skills and strategies that will help you tell the best story possible while exploring your own creativity and developing a storytelling process that works for you. But most importantly, I hope this book will inspire and motivate you to finish the stories you've started, begin exciting new stories, and get your stories in front of readers.

Some examples in this book contain spoilers. For a full list of books, movies, and television shows referenced, see the works cited section.

Part One: The Core Elements of Storytelling

1

Characters

We see ourselves in a story's characters. We see people we know—people we love, people we hate, people we fear, and people we want to emulate.

We love characters, loathe them, judge them, take their sides, or stand in opposition to them. We cheer them on and boo them. We celebrate them, and sometimes we mourn them. We form relationships with them, even though they're just figments of some storyteller's imagination.

Characters are the heart and soul of a story. We care about a story only to the extent that we care about its characters. In order for us to connect with characters, they need to do more than move the plot forward. Characters require depth and complexity. Who are these characters? What do they want? Why do they want it? What's standing in their way? Realistic characters come with all the flaws, quirks, and baggage that real people possess. They're not just names on a page; they have pasts and personalities, and each one is unique.

Perhaps most importantly, characters must fit purposefully into the stories they inhabit.

Characters with Purpose

Ideally, every character plays a critical role, with each performing a function that is necessary to the story. When every character is essential, a story becomes tighter, more cohesive, and more compelling.

A character's function within a story can be significant, or it can be minor. In fact, it can be so minor that the character could be considered a prop rather than an active player in the story. If a scene takes place in a hospital, we'll likely encounter a doctor and a nurse. These characters might only get a line or two of dialogue. But they're present, because including them is necessary to the realism of the scene.

However, most characters in a story have a greater purpose than functioning as props, and the most compelling characters tend to perform a variety of functions within a story. In *The Wonderful Wizard of Oz*, the Scarecrow becomes a friend and companion to Dorothy, offering assistance as she journeys toward the Emerald City. He embodies a key trait that Dorothy must adopt: thoughtfulness (Dorothy tends to act before she thinks). The Scarecrow is Dorothy's ally and mentor and a symbolic representation of an attribute that Dorothy must attain in order to complete her journey. He's just one character, but he performs a multitude of functions that make him essential to the story.

A character can also play a minor but critical role in a story. Cinderella's Fairy Godmother only appears in a single scene, but she changes Cinderella's life forever. Without her Fairy Godmother, Cinderella never would have made it to the ball, and she never would have met her prince. The Fairy Godmother could have been used in other scenes—she could have shown up at the ball, or she could have been hanging around when the prince's entourage came looking for the owner of the glass slipper. But she appeared only when her presence was necessary to the story, and she's one of the most adored characters in the world.

Whether characters appear frequently or occasionally,

each one must make a meaningful contribution to the story. In looking over a cast of characters, we should be able to pinpoint each one's purpose to the story.

Character Arcs

A character arc is a path of transformation. The story's events reshape the character's behavior, personality, worldview, or lifestyle, causing the character to change.

Most character arcs involve growth; characters undergo positive development over the course of the story and end up wiser, stronger, or better off in some meaningful way. We like to see characters improve themselves, because it means we can change for the better too. And the idea that there's hope for us—that we could improve ourselves or our circumstances, even through a series of difficult challenges, is an attractive idea indeed.

Harry Potter starts out as an awkward, lonely orphan who is mistreated by his aunt, uncle, and cousin. But he emerges as a great and powerful wizard. Yet it's not wizardry that makes Harry Potter great and powerful. It's the commitment, courage, and kindness that he develops throughout the course of the story. The choices he makes through every step of his journey determine the course of his character's evolution.

However, an arc can take a negative trajectory, in which case a character worsens over time. For example, a character who is good turns bad. An example would be Anakin Skywalker's journey toward becoming Darth Vader in the *Star Wars* franchise.

Character arcs primarily affect the protagonist, but other characters can undergo transformation too, making a story more dynamic. Some readers identify with supporting characters more than the protagonist, and when these characters grow and change, the story becomes more satisfying for more readers.

Do all stories include characters with arcs? Not necessarily. Plot-driven narratives often feature protagonists who don't evolve. The characters are there to guide us through the plot. An example would be a series of police procedurals, in which each story is focused on solving a crime. The principal characters, who are cops, rarely undergo fundamental change, although longer story arcs may depict some character development.

Character arcs often begin with two key elements: an external goal and an internal struggle. This combination of goal and struggle often forms the basis for the plot as well as the character arc. Katniss Everdeen's external goal is to survive the Hunger Games, but she is inhibited by her internal struggle: she doesn't want to kill innocent people. Yet the only way to survive the games is to kill her opponents. Stories that center around a character approaching a goal while wrestling with an internal struggle that prohibits them from reaching that goal result in plots that are emotionally gripping and characters who are deeply sympathetic.

A character's goal and struggle may change as the story progresses. Harry Potter starts out wanting love and acceptance, but once he gets love and acceptance, he develops a new goal: to save the wizard world from the evil Lord Voldemort.

Characters with clear and distinct arcs are perhaps the most powerful characters of all, and you can find these characters in every type of story. They can be memorable and iconic, but sometimes they're subtle and nuanced. They appear in quiet works of literary fiction and loud, action-packed adventures.

Character Classification

In order to better understand how characters fit into stories, we can classify them in various ways. Some classifications tell us the character's role or function in the story (for example, the protagonist is the main character). Other classifications tell us how prominent the character is among fellow cast mates (primary versus secondary characters).

Protagonists

The protagonist is the main character in a story. The main character isn't always easy to identify, especially when the supporting characters get a lot of screen time, undergo character arcs, and play important roles in the story. In these cases, the protagonist can be identified as the character who the story is happening to, who makes difficult choices, and who undergoes a meaningful and personal change. It's the character at the center of the conflict who is pursuing a clearly defined goal, often a primal goal, such as surviving or finding love.

A hero is a common type of protagonist, someone who is seeking justice. But the protagonist doesn't have to be a hero. The protagonist can be an antihero, someone who is viewed as evil or just plain unlikable. However, the protagonist might be neither a hero nor an antihero but someone who possesses a mix of good and bad traits.

Antagonists

The antagonist is quite literally antagonizing the protagonist. It's a common misconception that an antagonist is a villain or "bad guy." It's true that villains are a type of antagonist, but an antagonist is merely the force that is at odds with whatever the protagonist is trying to achieve.

In a story where the protagonist is trying to get a promotion, the antagonist could be a perfectly nice person who is up for the same job but who is also trying hard to get it. An antagonist doesn't even have to be a character. In a disaster story, the antagonist is the storm, the tornado, or the asteroid hurtling toward Earth. And occasionally, the protagonist and the antagonist are one and the same, when the force preventing the protagonist from achieving the goal is the self.

Primary Characters

Primary characters (often called main characters) are those with leading roles, including the protagonist. They dominate the scenes and are in the center of the action. The story is happening to them; they are actively causing events to unfold or reacting to situations that arise.

Depending on the narrative point of view, primary characters are likely to be viewpoint characters, meaning we see the story through their eyes and experience it along with them.

Secondary Characters

Secondary characters have a less significant influence on the events of a story. They appear in fewer scenes than primary characters, usually subplots and backstories. However, they play essential roles and often make repeat appearances.

Tertiary Characters

Tertiary characters (sometimes called supplemental characters) are relatively insignificant to the events of a story and often function more as props than people. These are characters who the primary and secondary characters must encounter, often passively: the server at a restaurant, the clerk at a grocery story, the other passengers on a bus. Tertiary characters are often unnamed and have minimal or zero effect on the plot.

The lines between primary, secondary, and tertiary characters are blurry, and many characters are difficult to classify. However, these classifications allow us to view the characters in a hierarchal structure so that we can understand their importance to the story relative to the other characters.

Stock Characters

Stock characters are those characters who we see frequently in stories—the gum-popping waitress, the wise guy, the mad scientist, the boy or girl next door. These characters feel familiar to readers, but they're tricky to pull off because they often feel clichéd. They work well in minor roles or when they're given a fresh twist. Stock characters are often confused with stereotypes.

Stereotypical Characters

Stereotypes are widely held views about people, usually

demographic groups. These views can be positive or negative. However, the broad effect of stereotypes is almost always negative because they assume that one thing is true about an entire group of people when, in fact, plenty of people within the group do not embody the attribute assigned to them. An example of a stereotype would be the starving artist, an assumption that it's impossible to make a good living as an artist; therefore, all artists must be poor.

In creating characters, it's usually best to avoid stereotypes. Stereotypical characters feel like carbon copies of characters we've seen too many times. They are misrepresentative and can be offensive to people within certain demographic groups.

Archetypal Characters

Archetypes are characters who reflect universal symbols, roles, and relationships. Unlike stock characters or stereotypes, there is a universal quality to archetypes. Their traits or their functions in a story are essential. Archetypes don't have to be characters; themes, symbols, and settings can be archetypes as well. However, a character most commonly fulfills the function of an archetype. As with stock characters, these characters can come off as clichés if they are poorly designed.

Carl Jung was a Swiss psychologist who identified numerous archetypes and defined them as belonging to the human collective unconscious; they're universal because they occur across cultures and throughout history. Some examples of common character archetypes identified by Jung include the following: innocent, orphan, hero, caregiver, explorer, rebel, lover, creator, jester, sage, magician, and ruler. As you can see, these archetypes mostly point to the roles that characters play (caregiver) in a story or key traits that they embody (innocent), not their behaviors or personalities.

Mythologist Joseph Campbell discovered the Monomyth (or Hero's Journey), a universal story pattern that is packed with archetypal characters. His work was heavily influenced by Jung. As a result, the Hero's Journey story structure includes eight archetypes: Hero, Herald, Mentor, Threshold Guardian, Shadow, Shapeshifter, Trickster, and Allies. We'll explore the Hero's Journey in greater detail in a future chapter.

Ensembles

It's often assumed that every story contains a protagonist and an antagonist, but this isn't always true. Ensemble stories feature a cast of characters who hold equal importance. Ensembles are especially popular on television but can also be found in books and movies. The television show *Friends* featured a group of twenty-somethings in New York City navigating their careers, love lives, and friendships. Each of the characters held equal importance. Therefore, all six main characters were protagonists.

Ensembles are often episodic, and members of the ensemble will step into the lead role for any given episode. In this sense, the larger story is an ensemble, but the characters take turns playing the lead in various installments.

A true ensemble would be the film *The Breakfast Club*, which is about five high school students spending a Saturday in detention. All of them undergo a parallel and simultaneous journey of self-discovery. There is no single protagonist in the film; the members of the ensemble are all protagonists.

Casts

Characters are individuals, but in a story they're also part of a larger group. The characters need to fit together like a puzzle, each performing a particular function in the story but also holding a distinct place within the group dynamics.

A cast will feel like a crowd of clones if each character isn't unique. Depending on the context, there are a variety of ways that characters can be distinct from one another. The most distinguishing features that separate characters from one another are their personalities, attitudes, and behaviors. But characters can also come from diverse cultures, cliques, or socioeconomic backgrounds.

Diversity is an important consideration for any cast of characters. If the cast doesn't reflect reality, the story will suffer from being unbelievable. Consider a story that takes place at a big office building in a large, coastal American city. In order to be realistic, the cast should be diverse in terms of ethnicity, gender, religion, and political affiliation. Giving each character their own arc with individual goals, struggles, and motivations is another way to distinguish them.

A character's function in a story also differentiates them from the other characters. One character might push the story toward conflict while another tries to avoid it. Duplicate characters are best avoided: in a story where a group of friends are trapped in a basement, we don't need two plumbers. Stories need characters who complement one another but also conflict with one another. They should balance one another out.

Relationships between the characters tend to be a huge draw for audiences. Characters need to have chemistry. Some relationships are harmonious, while others are fraught with friction. And the most interesting relationships are a mix of harmony and discord. Even characters who hate one another have chemistry; it's negative chemistry, but it's chemistry nonetheless. A combination of dynamic relationships results in a rich and interesting cast.

Tips for Creating Dynamic Characters

- **Backstory.** We're born a certain way, but our life experiences continually mold and shape us. Each character has a life before the story begins, and the author should have knowledge of each character's history.

- **Dialogue and behavior.** From the way they talk to how they behave, each character should be distinct. Make sure characters don't sound and act alike.

- **Physical description.** Our primary method of identifying one another is the way we look; hair and eye color, height and weight, scars and tattoos, and the style of clothing we wear are all part of our physical descriptions.

- **Name.** *Esmeralda* doesn't sound like a soccer mom, and *Joe* doesn't sound like an evil sorcerer. Make sure the names you choose for your characters match their personalities and the roles they play in the story. This will make them more memorable.

- **Goals.** Some say that characters' goals drive the entire story. He wants to slay the dragon; she wants to overthrow the evil empire. Goals can be small (the character wants a new car) or big (the character is trying to save the world). Just about every character in a story has a goal.

- **Internal and external struggles.** Characters who easily achieve their goals aren't very interesting, which is why we need antagonists. However, the most riveting struggles come from within. A character who can't go to college because it's not in the budget isn't as interesting as a character who doesn't go to college because she feels obligated to stay home and take care of a sick family member. However, a character who can't afford college and who also feels obligated to stay home is even more interesting, because she's dealing with two struggles, one internal and one external, both of which are preventing her from achieving her goal.

- **Strengths and weaknesses.** Villains sometimes do nice things, and heroes occasionally take the low road. What are your characters' most positive and negative behaviors and personality traits?

- **Friends and family.** These are the people in our inner circles, and they play important roles in shaping our personalities and our lives. Who are your characters' friends and family before the story starts? What new friends will they meet once the story begins?

- **Nemesis.** A nemesis is someone with whom we are at odds. This character doesn't have to be a villain, but the goals of the nemesis definitely interfere with your character's goals.

- **Position in the world.** What do your characters do for a living? What are their daily lives like? Where do they live? What is a character's role or position among their friends, family, or coworkers?

- **Skills and abilities.** Characters' skills and abilities can get them out of a tight spot or prevent them from being able to get out of a tight spot. What skills and training do your characters have? What skills and training do they lack? Will they acquire those skills?

- **Purpose and function.** Can you identify a purpose for every character in a story? Do some characters perform one function while others perform multiple functions?

- **Fears.** An old fiction writing trick is to figure out what your character is most afraid of, and then make the character face it. Give each character a fear, even if they never face it in the story.

- **Cast review.** Review your characters as a cast, and look at them in smaller groups and other couplings. Do they complement and contrast with one another? Is there built-in chemistry (positive or negative)?

2

Plot

A plot is a sequence of related events in a story. Plot is not to be confused with structure, which determines how the events unfold, the order in which scenes are placed, and the characters' roles within the story.

Plot usually centers around the protagonist's primary goal or challenge, the central story problem. Each event in the story pushes the protagonist toward a climax where they either succeed or fail to resolve the story problem. In a mystery, the challenge might be to solve a crime. In a romance, the goal is to find true love.

The events that make up a plot are called plot points—the actions and reactions that give a story momentum. The killer strikes, an investigation launches. A clue is found, the detective hauls in a suspect. The suspect alibis out, the detective is back to square one. Each event leads to the next. Plot points are like wheels on a bus; they keep the story rolling forward.

As the plot progresses, the stakes get higher and tensions rise. A killer is on the loose. If the detective doesn't solve the crime fast, the killer will strike again. As the detective closes in, the killer taunts the detective and threatens his family. Then he kidnaps the detective's daughter. The situation grows increasingly dire, desperate, or dangerous. The story intensifies at every turn.

The climax is the moment in the story where tension

reaches its peak and the stakes are maxed out. The climax occurs near the end of the story and is followed by a resolution, which is when the central story problem (main plot) and all subplots are resolved. Getting to the climax isn't easy for the characters; otherwise, there would be no story to tell. Therefore, the journey is hard on them, causing a lot of suffering. This results in a satisfying payoff at the story's end.

The suffering that characters endure as they move through a plot is relative. In a mystery, the detective may end up in the hospital with a gunshot wound, on the brink of death. In a romance, the suffering could be more emotional and less existential, with the protagonist coping with loneliness or rejection.

It might seem that a simple way to keep raising stakes and tension in a story is to increase the characters' suffering. Every scene, every chapter, can show the protagonist's situation getting worse and worse. This certainly has been done, but life is a series of ups and downs, and the most compelling stories reflect real life. Characters face some setbacks and losses but also enjoy some successes along the way.

In a tightly woven plot, all events are necessary and intertwined with the central conflict. Removing any scene or plot point would break the story. If characters are running around (or sitting around) doing things that don't move the plot forward, the story will drag. Readers lose interest when a story is filled with unnecessary excess: backstory that isn't relevant to the plot, lengthy exposition about how a gadget works, and pages of description become tedious. Most readers don't want to drift too far from the plot, get pulled out of the story, or be confused by tangents.

However, plots that are more loosely structured resonate well with some readers. Backstories, in-depth detail, and lengthy descriptions are acceptable—if not mandatory—in some genres. For example, hard science fiction demands accurate and detailed explanations of the science or technology within the story. Historical novels and fantasies are rich with description, which helps set the scene and bring readers into the story world.

Genre can also dictate the events in a story and direction of the plot. Although most genre rules and tropes involve tone and setting, many are relevant to plot. Romance stories are always about a romantic pursuit or entanglement and always have a happy ending. Mysteries always involve a puzzle of some kind, usually solving a crime. Most (but not all) science fiction explores the benefits or drawbacks of scientific advancements. So we know certain plot points will appear in certain genres. One of the many reasons it's critical for authors to read in their genres is to learn these rules in order to ensure that their plots fulfill readers' basic expectations.

Readers keep turning pages for two reasons: they care about the characters, and they want to find out what happens. When a plot is well crafted, readers will stick around, because they want to see the detective catch the killer, or they want to see the protagonist find love.

Subplots

Subplot is short for subordinate plot, a secondary or supporting story. Most stories include multiple subplots. These may or may not be intertwined with or related to the main plot; however, stories tend to feel more cohesive when everything is tied together. Subplots can stretch through the entire story, or they can occupy shorter blocks.

Subplots work exactly like plots, except they are less significant. Secondary characters are often at the helm of subplots; in this sense, they're like miniature stories within the larger story but with other characters stepping into the role of protagonist.

Subplots can fulfill a variety of functions within a story: deepening or expanding the central plot, providing insight into key characters, showing how various and complex components of the central plot tie together. And subplots are often large or extensive plot points. For example, a subplot might extend through three chapters of a novel, acting as both a story within a story and a plot point for the primary story.

Stories with subplots feel more complex and dynamic, giving readers more to digest, and they work well when closely related to the main plot.

Plot Types and Originality

It's not uncommon for writers to develop a premise, concept, or entire plot only to realize that something similar has already been done. It's tempting to throw the idea away and search for something more original. In some cases, that might be a smart move. But most of the time, throwing away an "unoriginal" idea is a mistake.

Writers who worry endlessly about whether their plots are original get stuck in an infinite cycle of searching for some idea that has never been done before.

Plots are built around conflict, but there are only a few conflicts to choose from. There is some debate about how many conflicts exist. Some traditions argue for three; others identify four or more. Here's a list of six:

- Man vs. man
- Man vs. nature
- Man vs. society
- Man vs. self
- Man vs. machine
- Man vs. supernatural

That's it. The central conflict of every plot is based on one of these conflicts. Examine any story you can think of, and you'll be able to classify it as one of these six conflicts.

Within these conflicts, we can come up with many different types of plots and a wide variety of event sequences. For example, in man versus nature, one story might be about a character coping with an illness while another could be about a group of friends surviving a devastating hurricane.

However, we can also demonstrate that these plots are just as unoriginal as the conflict they're based on. In his book *The Seven Basic Plots: Why We Tell Stories*, journalist and author Christopher Booker identified the following seven plot types:

- Overcoming the monster: the hero attempts to defeat an evil or antagonistic force.

- Rags to riches: a poor protagonist attempts to acquire wealth.

- The quest: the hero sets out on a journey to find a significant item or treasure.

- Voyage and return: the protagonist embarks on a long voyage to a distant place, faces a series of threats, and then returns home.

- Comedy: in the traditional sense, the only requirement for a comedy is a happy ending; however, comedy usually implies a lighthearted and funny spectacle with a triumphant ending.

- Tragedy: a tragedy is usually about the downfall (and often death) of a character or cast of characters.

- Rebirth: the protagonist is forced to change his or her ways.

Although these plot types can be literal, they can also be metaphorical. A rags-to-riches story may not deal explicitly with material wealth. Romance stories in which the protagonists are lonely and looking for love would be classified as rags-to-riches stories: love is the wealth the protagonist wants to acquire. *Cinderella* is an example of a story that blends both a literal rags-to-riches plot with a metaphorical one—because she gains material wealth, and she finds love.

Plenty of stories contain more than one plot type; in fact, rebirth is common in many of the other plots.

Think of all the books you've read and movies you've watched. Can you think of any with a plot that doesn't fit into one of these plot types? Probably not, and that's why trying to be original is a useless task.

If there are only a few conflicts and plots to choose from, then why do some stories feel original? Because they use old ideas that are presented in new ways, often by combining plots, characters, settings, and themes in unique and unexpected ways.

Tips for Devising a Compelling Plot

- **Goals and motives.** Build a plot around the protagonist's goals. What does the hero want? What does the antagonist want? What do the other characters want? Why do the characters want these things? Goals and motives are the driving forces behind the characters' actions and decisions.

- **Conflict.** What's preventing the protagonist from achieving their goal? Story is very much about conflict. Look for ways to insert conflict into the story at every level from the strife of the central plot to minor clashes between characters.

- **Stakes.** Tensions rise and stakes get higher as the plot unfolds. What will the characters gain if they succeed? What will they lose if they fail?

- **Momentum.** Make sure every scene and chapter move the plot forward in a meaningful way. If a scene can be cut without changing the story, then that scene is unnecessary.

- **Genre.** Be aware of your genre so that you can include the appropriate plot points (if applicable).

- **Plot versus character.** Avoid plots that overshadow the characters, and avoid characters who do little more than guide readers through the plot. A good balance of compelling characters and a gripping plot results in the best possible story.

- **Originality.** Don't worry about being original. Focus on developing fresh ideas for your story. Use the other elements—characters, setting, and theme—to enrich your plot and make it feel innovative.

- **Subplots.** Build in subplots that are connected to the main plot.

- **Conflict and plot types.** Using the conflict and plot types listed in this chapter, identify which conflicts and plots are in your story. Does your story include multiple conflicts and plots?

- **Resolution.** When you finish your draft, make a list of the subplots. Are all subplots and the central plot resolved in a satisfactory way? If you're planning to write a sequel, did you close the main plot but leave a story thread open?

- **Plotting and planning.** Making a list of your plot points gives you a good overview of your story, which you can quickly review to check for flow, pacing, conflict, and tension.

- **Page-turners.** Not all stories are page-turners, but if your goal is to keep readers glued to the story, plan plot points that intrigue and entice them.

3

Setting

Setting may not seem as critical to a story as character or plot, yet it is a core element of storytelling and for good reason. The setting of a story helps us understand where and when it takes place, which gives the story context. If the audience doesn't have a sense of setting, they'll feel lost and confused (sometimes that might be the author's intent).

A setting can be big or small. It can be a made-up world—a massive galaxy with multiple star systems and inhabited planets—or it can be a single room—four walls and a ceiling.

Settings can offer opportunities or present limitations for the characters. For example, when an apocalyptic event occurs, characters in a big city loot stores and warehouses, but food runs out fast and eventually people head for the hills. If the story is set in the farmlands, characters might not face an immediate food shortage. In fact, their biggest challenge might come later, when the city folk show up and attempt to hijack their crops. The setting of the story therefore drives the action, even if only peripherally.

Some settings provide conflict for a story. A story about a natural disaster, such as a tornado, must take place in a region where tornadoes are likely to strike. An author might choose a setting because it offers certain types of conflict for the characters. In the earlier apocalyptic example, an author might want to tell a story with looting and fighting and will therefore set the story in a metropolitan area. Other times, a setting is chosen at random but affects the course of the story nonetheless. For example, if a story is set in the mountains, when an emergency arises, it will likely take a lot longer for emergency services to arrive than if the story is set in the suburbs.

Tone and mood are also affected by a story's setting. Consider a story set during the summer at a bright, sunny beach resort versus a story set during a dark, stormy winter at an old, abandoned Victorian mansion.

A story's setting will also determine the culture in which the characters are immersed. The attitudes, behaviors, and lifestyles of characters in a desert village are going to differ wildly from those of characters living along the coast of a small island.

Where and when we live has a profound influence on our lives. The experience of growing up in suburban America during the twentieth century is radically different from growing up in Ancient Egypt. Living in Europe during the Middle Ages would have been different from the experience of living there today.

Depending on the time and place, the characters' experiences may differ based on their race, gender, or sexual orientation. For example, life was more difficult for women in the West before they could vote.

And some stories are all about the setting, meaning they're quite literally about a particular time and place, even more than they're about the characters or plot. Many historical novels give readers the experience of what it was like to live during a different time and place. Science-fiction and fantasy stories do the same but are based on imaginings or forecasts rather than on historical research.

Some settings function as little more than backdrops—although even a backdrop is critical. These settings may require very little work on a storyteller's part (because they're based on the contemporary real world) compared to settings that involve elaborate research or world building. Some settings are so seamlessly integrated into a story that we don't even notice them. Others are so distinct and active that they function as characters within a story.

The *Harry Potter* books are rich with many magical settings, but Hogwarts, the school for wizards, often feels more like a character than a location. It's a setting that feels alive; the characters interact with it and develop relationships with it. Setting as character is not limited to fantasy, science fiction, or horror. The television show *Sex and the City* is often hailed for making New York City the fifth character in the ensemble, and the island on the television show *Lost* was very much a character in the series.

It can be exciting for readers to discover a place they're familiar with in a fictional story. Michael Connelly's Harry Bosch novels often take readers through streets, past parks, and into real neighborhoods throughout Los Angeles. This is especially effective in big, coastal cities where a lot of readers may live or have visited.

The details of a contemporary or real-world setting must be accurate. If a reader in France feels a depiction of Paris is inaccurate, it could hurt the story's believability. As with all aspects of a story, the setting must be vivid, realistic, and believable, even if it's made up.

For greatest ease, authors can use their hometowns and nearby cities as models for the settings in their stories, which alleviates the need to travel or conduct research that might otherwise be necessary to get the setting right.

However, some stories necessitate distant locations, and in such cases travel could become extremely helpful, depending on the level of detail the setting needs. Often it's the smallest details that make a setting vivid and bring it to life, especially those details that one only observes with hands-on experience. In addition, the overall tone and atmosphere can be difficult to achieve without having visited a place.

It's not always possible to visit a location. Plenty of authors write stories set in places they've never visited in person. In these cases, research is essential. Books and documentaries as well as other stories that take place in these settings are vital research materials, as are modern tools, such as the Internet, which we can use to view live and interactive maps. And of course, interviewing residents or showing drafts to people familiar with the setting are excellent ways to capture the realism of a place.

Some stories may not require a deep level of research. Plenty of authors use made-up towns, and these can be based on an accessible location. If we live near a small town, we can use it as a model for the small town in our story, but we can also alter it to suit our needs. If the real small town doesn't have a big, creepy haunted house, we can always add one.

Although historical settings were once real, they have changed over time, so visiting them offers a limited sense of what things were like in the past. The people, cultures, and structures are long gone, which means developing a realistic historical setting will require a lot of in-depth research in order to understand the culture, the geography, and even the props—everyday items that characters use in the stories.

Time is especially important in a historical setting because culture changes over time. The laws, customs, and beliefs of people in a single location will vary depending on the year in which a story is set. Stories must align with historical events. It would be awkward to read a story set in Paris around 1789 without including the upheaval of the French Revolution.

Settings are primarily established through description, action, and dialogue. Description is the simplest and most common way to relay a setting to a reader. But some readers will nod off if forced to sludge through pages (or even paragraphs) of description. Modern audiences like to get to the action and dialogue—they want to know what's happening.

While paragraphs of description can establish a setting, action and dialogue can also be used to bring readers into a story world. Characters interact with the world around them, and they talk about it, which means setting can be incorporated into action and dialogue, as long as it's natural to the story.

For example, instead of using description to explain the furnishings in a room, the characters can sit in plush velvet chairs or lean on rickety tables. One character might make a remark about a Picasso painting that's hanging on the wall; another might admire the white linen draperies. If a character asks another character to go to the movies, we know the story is set in the twentieth century or later. When those characters watch a hologram, we know it's set in the future.

World Building: Historical and Speculative Fiction

World building extends beyond the location in which a story is set; it includes everything from the climate and culture to the everyday items that the characters use.

Settings in speculative fiction (sci-fi, fantasy, and some horror) offer world-building opportunities that allow authors to engage their imaginations. While these genres can be set in the real world (past or present), the vast majority of speculative stories take readers to far-off, futuristic, and fantastical locations that come from mythology or the author's own imagination.

Some authors go to great lengths to get the details of their speculative settings just right, ensuring that their world building is clear, consistent, and believable. This requires attention to detail and consistency in everything from the look and feel of the world to the culture, customs, and language. And here, again, authors might conduct extensive research that informs and inspires their story worlds, perhaps even visiting foreign locations that can be used as inspiration for a fantastical or futuristic setting.

Science fiction is often concerned with the future. We can research projections and scholarly works by futurists to get a sense of what the future might look like, but nobody knows for sure what the future holds. Developing an understanding of history is surprisingly useful for creating futuristic worlds. By understanding the trajectory of human culture and technology, it's a little easier to make a believable guess about what the world might look like in fifty, a hundred, or a thousand years.

Fantasy stories don't always take place in made-up

worlds. In fact, many epic fantasy stories are set in worlds that are loosely based on Medieval Europe, and plenty of urban or paranormal fantasy stories are set in the modern world. However, these stories add new elements to the world by changing the rules of reality—they add magic to the mix as well as fantastical creatures ranging from fairies and unicorns to trolls and dragons. The rules of such magic systems are key components of world building in the fantasy genre.

Authors often use a story bible, which helps them keep track of the various elements of their stories, especially their story worlds. The story bible can include descriptions of locations, timelines, and maps. It's a simple tool that authors can reference any time they need to fact-check the structure or rules of their made-up worlds. Story bibles are especially valuable for writing series, because after a few books, keeping track of hundreds (or thousands) of details can get cumbersome.

Tips for Designing a Vivid Setting

- **It's all in the details.** Details make a setting pop. Climate, geography, architecture, and culture make a setting realistic.

- **Use a model.** When creating a made-up setting, use a real location as a model, but let your imagination reshape the location, turning it into a new world. If possible, use your city or a nearby town as a model; this gives you easy access.

- **Research.** When using a real location as a setting (or a model), conduct as much research as you can. Try to visit the location. Talk to locals, and peruse images and videos of the location online. Read books and watch movies about it.

- **Time.** The time in which a story takes place is a major component of the setting. Over time, everything changes from the customs to the technology. Double-check your facts if you're writing historical fiction, and use history as a trajectory when you're writing about the future.

- **Changing settings.** Your story may take place in multiple settings. Move your story through time and space with smooth transitions. Use markers to let readers know where and when each scene is taking place.

- **Setting as character.** Is the setting vivid enough to function as a character within the story? Do the characters talk about it frequently? Does it have an especially big influence on their lives or the story? Could this story take place in any other location?

- **Establishing the setting.** Although large blocks of description about the setting are sometimes necessary, try to reveal details about the setting through action and dialogue. Avoid constantly stating the time or date. Drop clues, such as a setting sun or a snowy field, which establish the setting clearly but subtly.

- **Props.** Props are the everyday items that characters encounter in a story's setting. From swords and petticoats to microchips and hovercars, the props in a story often play a big role in bringing the setting to life in the reader's mind, especially in speculative fiction.

- **World building.** If you're building a world from scratch, keep the facts and details consistent. Readers will notice if the rules of the world are incongruous. If you're writing an epic story or a series, keep track of the details of your world in a story bible.

4

Theme

Theme is one of the most difficult story elements to understand. Often confused with plot, theme is actually a worldview, philosophy, message, moral, ethical question, or lesson. However, these labels, taken alone or together, don't quite explain theme in fiction.

We can think of a theme as an underlying principle or concept, the topic at the center of the story.

Themes are often universal in nature. Some common universal themes are based on motifs of redemption, freedom, equality, sacrifice, betrayal, loyalty, greed, justice, oppression, revenge, and love. Themes can also be personal and part of the human condition. Such themes could explore issues surrounding loneliness, trust, commitment, or family.

However, a story's theme is more than an idea that can be expressed in a single word. The concept of freedom can form the foundation of a story's theme, which could be anything from "one should not sacrifice freedom for security" to "freedom is worth dying for."

Themes can be philosophical, asking ethical questions or pitting two ideas against each other: science versus faith, good versus evil, why are we here, and what happens when we die?

A story doesn't need to answer the ethical questions it raises through its theme; in fact, many readers prefer stories that show both sides of a thematic argument, allowing readers to make up their own minds. Stories that do attempt to answer ethical question can come across as preachy, which is suitable in a children's book but usually falls flat in stories for adults.

Themes can also present warnings, which is often the case with speculative fiction. The theme of George Orwell's *1984* is wrapped around a totalitarian government that uses technology to spy on and control its citizens. In this case, the totalitarian government is shown as an evil social construct, and only one side of that argument is offered, probably because there is universal agreement that totalitarianism is bad for humanity.

Most stories contain multiple themes and motifs; *The Hunger Games* trilogy explores motifs of power, class, sacrifice, and honor, to name a few. In the *Harry Potter* books, the most significant themes are good versus evil and the power of love. However, there are also motifs of friendship and loyalty. One theme might stretch across an entire series, while other themes appear at the novel or even chapter level. A story's main plot might explore one theme while its subplots explore other themes.

The strongest stories tend to use themes that are interconnected and complement or contrast with one another. The 1997 film *Titanic* is rich with themes that swirl around class (wealth versus poverty). These themes are echoed in the main characters: the protagonist is an aristocrat; she falls in love with a poor artist. The ship itself is segregated with the wealthy residing on the luxurious upper decks and the poor relegated to the cramped and crowded accommodations in the lower decks. And at the center of the story, the protagonist, Rose, is struggling with whether she should give up her financial security in order to liberate herself from the wealthy fiancé she loathes.

Thematic patterning occurs when there is a recurring motif in a story that supports and reinforces the theme. In the original *Star Wars* trilogy, thematic patterning suggests that nature is preferable to technology. The good characters are often seen in organic settings: the desert, the snow, a forest; whereas the evil characters are almost always aboard a spaceship. When they do touch down on a planet, the stormtroopers are decked out in armor, so they never truly interact with a natural environment. And the story's villain, Darth Vader, is more machine than man.

Theme can be obvious, but often it's nuanced. In the 2009 film *Avatar*, the theme is in your face: preservation of the environment and respect for native cultures. In the 2005 film *Batman Begins*, theme is harder to put your finger on: one man's struggle with his own identity and duality.

Themes can be difficult to identify—not only because there are often multiple themes in a work but also because two people might interpret two different themes. One person might identify the theme of savagery versus civility in *Lord of the Flies*, while another person might identify a theme based on survival. Sometimes there's no right or wrong answer, and that's the magic of art and the beauty of theme: it's up to each individual to find their own meaning in it.

Themes are so closely tied to human nature that it's almost impossible to tell a story without a theme of some kind. Themes will almost always manifest, even if an author doesn't put any special effort into theme development.

Some experts have suggested that authors shouldn't think too much about theme until they've produced a draft, while others believe that theme is so integral that it should be present throughout story development. The approach you choose will depend on your writing process, storytelling style, and personal preference.

Theme could be considered the glue that holds a story together, the binding principle of the narrative. It is the deeper meaning, the truth that underscores the plot and characters.

Tips for Developing Theme

- **Learn to identify themes.** When watching movies and reading novels, identify the themes. When you become proficient at identifying themes in other works, you'll get better at bringing themes into your own work.

- **Don't stress yet.** If you're not sure what your story's theme is, don't put too much pressure on yourself. A theme will usually emerge as you work through your first draft.

- **Theme development.** Once you've completed a draft, the theme should be apparent. Take some time to think about how you can strengthen the theme in future drafts.

- **Multiple themes.** Once you identify your theme, make a list of related themes that you could thread into subplots. For example, if your theme is related to redemption, then forgiveness could be a secondary theme.

- **Theme starters.** If you'd like to build a story around a theme, make a list of themes that you're interested in exploring, and use them to inspire ideas for plots and characters.

- **Theme and character.** Look for ways you can use characters to represent the themes in your story. For example, one character could be seeking redemption while another character needs to learn how to forgive.

- **Assess the execution of your theme.** Is your theme coming across as preachy? If your theme is two-sided (science versus faith, for example), have you fairly represented both sides in your story?

- **Theme and motif.** Check your work by making a list of all motifs and themes in your story. This is a map of your thematic pattern.

Part Two: Narrative

5

Style, Voice, and Tone

Literary style is the aesthetic quality of a work of literature—the distinct voice that makes each author unique. It's the way we string words together, the rhythm of our prose, the catchphrases that pepper our language. Literary style includes every element of writing in which an author can make stylistic choices from syntax and grammar to character and plot development.

Seasoned writers have cultivated a style of writing that can be identified by a snippet of prose alone. For example, a common English literature test gives you excerpts from several authors whose works you've studied. The challenge is to identify the author who wrote each excerpt—not because you've memorized each author's repertoire but to show that you can identify each author by his or her voice.

Style can be contained in a single work, such as a novel, or it can be observed across an author's entire body of work. One author's style might be spartan—minimalistic in nature—while another author's style is rich with vibrant language. An author can also exhibit a range of styles, adjusting the aesthetics for each project, depending on what works best for each piece.

Style is comprised of many components. However, it is not any one component; nor is it all of these components together. Each author (or work) uses a unique combination of components to render a style. Among these components are personality, tone, diction, syntax, grammar, and content.

The term *voice* is often used interchangeably with *style*, but voice is more specific to an author's prosaic personality—diction (vocabulary choice) and syntax (sentence structure). Think about the people you know and the way they talk. Each of them frequently uses certain words and phrases. Their speech may have a particular rhythm or cadence. They may even be consistent in tone—optimistic, pessimistic, or somewhere in between. That's voice.

A narrative voice often echoes a real human personality, which can come from an author's natural personality. But voice can also be cultivated. Usually, it's a combination of natural personality and intentionally fine-tuning the language. The personality of an author's voice can be formal, witty, sarcastic, casual, or tense. It's the human feeling—the attitude—we get from the narrative.

Authors also make stylistic choices with grammar and punctuation. Cormac McCarthy is one such author who is known for his omission of punctuation marks. Most notably, he didn't use quotation marks for dialogue in his novel *The Road*. Nor did he use italics or any other punctuation marks or formatting to mark the dialogue. Dialogue was indicated within the context of the work.

Some authors are known for a style that resonates from the content or the substance of their works. These authors may always write about a particular type of character or topic. For example, one author might write stories that tackle social issues while another writes stories set in hospitals.

Style can also be expressed through structure. Some authors tell stories out of chronological order. Others may consistently use framing devices. Or maybe they're known for including flashbacks throughout their stories.

It's not unusual for young and new writers to ignore style. A fledgling storyteller often focuses on more concrete aspects of story, such as plot, character, and setting, along with other key elements like action, dialogue, and description. However, style is an important consideration, especially in literary fiction. In fact, style is one of the defining features of literary fiction, which is renowned for paying homage to the artistry of wordcraft. Some may even argue that the styling of prose and an author's voice are more important than the crafting of story in literary fiction.

Along with style and voice, tone gives a piece of writing its flavor. Tone is the emotional sensibility of a story. A horror story can be funny or creepy (or both). A romance novel can be whimsical or mysterious. A work of literary fiction can be joyful or sad. Whereas style and voice are more associated with the characteristics of a particular author's work, tone is associated with the way it makes readers feel.

However, tone is linked to style and voice, because many authors use a consistent tone throughout their works. Some authors are known for their dark humor or dry wit; others may be known for writing tearjerkers.

Tone doesn't require strict consistency. A horror story can be scary with some humorous moments. However, a story that is dark in tone with one or two moments of humor will feel off-kilter. Tone works well when it's consistent, and it needs to be balanced when it's not.

Style, voice, and tone work together to give an author's work its unique flavor. Readers often form preferences for stories with a particular stylistic quality and tonality. Some readers don't like dark stories and will only read stories with a light and casual vibe. Some may prefer fast-paced stories that are focused on action and dialogue, while others like to explore the details of a story world with vivid description and exposition. There are readers who like texts packed with long, fancy words and readers who prefer to skim the text rather than check the dictionary every few paragraphs (or pages).

Many readers may not even be aware of their own stylistic preferences. They'll scan the first few paragraphs and find something they like about the narrative voice (or something they don't like), which informs their decision to buy and read the book, which is why style, voice, and tone are important elements of storytelling.

6

Narrative: Point of View, Tense, and Pacing

The terms *story* and *narrative* can be used interchangeably, meaning a sequence of events, real or fictional, that are conveyed through any medium ranging from prose to film. However, when we talk about narrative, we're often referring to the structural nature or presentation of a story, the manner in which it's told.

Narrative Point of View

The narrator of a story is the in-world storyteller, the voice that imparts the story events to the audience. Narrative point of view, often called POV, determines the position of the narrator, relative to the story. Points of view include first person, second person, and third person.

If readers envision the events of a story as a movie playing in their minds, then the point of view is best described as where the camera is sitting at any given time. In the case of first-person point of view, the camera is inside the narrator's head; we see the story through their eyes. In limited third-person point of view, the camera sits on one character's shoulder; that character is not telling us the story, but we're close to their perspective of events. In omniscient third-person point of view, the camera is pulled back so it can capture everything in the story objectively.

First Person

In a first-person narrative, the narrator is a character within the story—often (but not always) an active participant. First-person point of view is easily identified by the narrator's use of *I* or *we*. It's often told from the point of view of the protagonist. *The Catcher in the Rye* is an example of a first-person narrative told from the protagonist's perspective. However, first-person narrative can also be relayed by a secondary or tertiary character, such as when the narrator is a witness to the story events rather than an active participant. In the case of a story such as *Heart of Darkness*, the first-person narrator is relaying a story as told to him by someone else.

The first-person point of view provides ample opportunities to present a narrator with a distinct voice, which flavors the story's tone, giving it personality and a subjective slant. For this reason, first-person narration can feel more intimate, as if the reader is in a close conversation with the storyteller. First person often feels as if we're inside the narrator's head. When executed well, this helps readers forge deep and lasting connections with the character and the story.

First person is ideal for stories that need to explore the narrator's internal thoughts and emotions. However, first-person narrative comes with interesting limitations, such as when the narrator is not privy to what other characters are thinking, feeling, or doing. Because some stories require that readers know what other characters are thinking and doing, first-person narration is not always appropriate.

Most first-person narratives are singular, told by one voice. Plural first-person narration would refer to the narrators as *we*, which is rare.

Stories can use multiple, singular first-person narrators, such as when chapters alternate between characters, all speaking from their own points of view. In such stories, it's critical to keep the jumps between characters clear and distinct, usually with scene breaks, chapter breaks, or headings that let readers know which character is speaking.

First-person narration is frequently used in all genres of fiction and is especially common in the nonfiction categories of memoir and autobiography.

Second Person

Second-person narratives use second-person personal pronouns (*you*) to refer to other characters or the reader. These stories often feel like the narrator is talking to the reader as if the reader is the main character in story. We tend to see second-person point of view used mostly in instructions ("After you dip the apples in caramel, set them on wax paper to harden."). This point of view is rarely used in storytelling. *Bright Lights, Big City* is one of the rare novels written in second person. Here's an excerpt:

> You keep thinking that with practice you will eventually get the knack of enjoying superficial encounters, that you will stop looking for the universal solvent, stop grieving. You will learn to compound happiness out of small increments of mindless pleasure.

Third Person

Third-person point of view is the most common form of prose narrative because it offers the greatest flexibility with access to all characters and full view of the story world and all events taking place. Even limited third-person narratives offer broader access to the story's full scope than a first-person narrative. Characters are referred to as *he*, *she*, and *they*. There is no *I* or *you*. The narrator is not a person but an entity.

Third-person narratives are categorized on two axes: subjective/objective and omniscient/limited.

Third-person subjective allows the narrator to describe characters' thoughts and feelings using internal dialogue. Third-person objective does not have access to characters' thoughts and feelings; it only offers an external view of the characters. Many narratives float in and out of subjective and objective, giving readers glimpses of the characters' thoughts when it benefits the story and keeping the characters' thoughts hidden when doing so serves the story.

A third-person omniscient narrative has full view of the story and characters at all times. The narrator knows everything in the story world but may choose which details to reveal to the reader. A third-person limited narrative only has full knowledge of one character and can only relay events that character is privy to.

Tense

Tense, or narrative time, determines whether the story takes place in the past, present, or future.

In past tense, the story has already happened; it's in the past. These stories are most easily identified by verbs that are in past tense. This is by far the most common tense for storytelling.

A present-tense story is happening now and feels immediate. Verbs are in present tense. *The Hunger Games* trilogy is written in first-person present tense:

> All the general fear I've been feeling condenses into an immediate fear of this girl, this predator who might kill me in seconds. Adrenaline shoots through me and I sling the pack over one shoulder and run full-speed for the woods.

Future tense is rare and relays events that will happen in the future.

Pacing

Pacing is the rhythm of a story—the underlying drumbeat that gives the reader a sense of timing. Some stories are fast paced while others move along at a leisurely pace. Pacing can speed up or slow down, depending on what's happening within the story. In fact, most stories pick up the pace as the climax approaches. A story with good pacing moves along at a smooth and comfortable clip.

Pacing should be consistent and relative, and in some stories, the action needs to intensify or speed up at certain points. For example, pacing might start out slow as we meet the characters and get to know them, but then it speeds up as they embark on their crazy adventure. If it takes a thousand words for the characters to plan an attack, the battle that follows should not be a mere five hundred words. This will cause the pacing to feel off balance. The battle is more important than the planning, and readers likely want to spend more time in battle than talking about it. Similarly, if a story builds up to a passionate love scene, that scene should last longer than a few paragraphs.

7

Action and Dialogue

Action and dialogue are the wheels that carry a story forward. The easiest way to imagine action and dialogue in written narrative is to think of a movie. When characters onscreen do things, that's action. When they talk, that's dialogue. Most of a story's momentum is contained in action and dialogue.

You may have heard the old writing adage "show, don't tell." It's one of those sayings that becomes blatantly obvious once you get it. Readers want to see what's happening. Characters walk and talk. They kick and punch and scratch. They cry and laugh, run and hide. They do things and say things. That's how story happens: through action and dialogue.

Back to "show, don't tell." What does it mean? Isn't storytelling the telling of a story? If we show it, then wouldn't it be a movie? Not quite. Here's an example: instead of telling readers that one character finds another character attractive, we can show the first character's heart racing, knees getting weak, and cheeks blushing.

When we show the story unfolding, it's easier for readers to visualize what's happening. It makes a story more visceral and immediate and therefore more compelling.

There are times when the narrative must use description and exposition to tell readers about certain parts of a story, but anything important that happens in the story is best played out through action and dialogue.

Action

Action can be an act contained within a single word: *chase*. It can be an entire scene that shows a character being chased down streets, through buildings, and then trapped in a corner. It can be threaded through dialogue as characters are talking to one another while they are being chased.

But action isn't always high octane. Action is an effective way to add realism to a story, such as when characters eat and drink while having a conversation. This type of action is most effective when it's carefully crafted to move the story forward in the best way possible.

Everything that characters do, from guzzling a beer to engaging in an epic battle, is action. Consider a scene where two characters are eating at a restaurant, having a conversation that is vital to the story. As they chat, they check out the other diners, look at their food, taste their food, and have a drink. All these actions can be used to take us deeper into the characters and the story. Is one character checking out the other diners, looking for someone they know? Are they worried they're being followed? Does a character eye the food with disgust or hunger? What food do they order? Are they drinking water or wine? Juice or beer? These choices will give the readers insight into the characters' personalities.

Many writers struggle with action scenes, especially scenes that show fighting and battles. These scenes are especially tricky to write if we've never been in a fight, no matter how many similar fights we've seen in movies.

While action scenes can be riveting, they become confusing if they're not well crafted and if the action is not crystal clear to the reader. When action is described in a simple yet vivid way, often step-by-step, the reader can follow along without straining or becoming confused. We've all read scenes in stories where we weren't sure exactly what was happening, and we may have read a passage a few times to figure out what was going on. Readers generally don't want to go through that in order to understand what's happening.

Action often intensifies as the story approaches the climax. The stakes get higher, things speed up. There are fewer casual chats in restaurants. Instead, there are heated arguments and fights, and all emotions are ratcheted up several notches. All of this is depicted through action that moves a little faster and is explained in language that adequately conveys not only what is happening but also how it's happening, and perhaps most importantly, how it feels.

When conveying action, word choice is critical. If a narrative says the characters ran to the other side of the street, we get a different visual than if it says they sprinted. And if they *fled* to the other side of the street, well, that's something else altogether.

Dialogue

Excellent dialogue can send a story soaring to new heights. Dialogue is an expression of the characters that reveals their personalities. Because character is where readers forge emotional connections with stories, well-crafted dialogue can deepen a reader's involvement with the characters, and by extension, the story.

Consider the following famous lines of dialogue from films and you'll begin to understand the power of dialogue:

"I've got a bad feeling about this." (*Star Wars*, 1977)

"Go ahead, make my day." (*Sudden Impact*, 1983)

"I'll have what she's having." (*When Harry Met Sally*, 1989)

Even if you haven't seen any of these movies, there's a good chance you're familiar with these quotes. When characters make witty quips and snazzy one-liners, they pop off the page and make the character and the moment memorable, sometimes to the point that a line of dialogue becomes embedded in our culture.

Dialogue can also boost characterization by making characters distinct through the way they talk. Characters from one country will have different expressions and language patterns than characters from another country. These patterns occur at more local levels as well. People from different regions—states, provinces, and cities—will use unique expressions and language patterns. If one character is from Texas and another is from California, they're going to speak differently from each other. Ensuring that these differences come though in a story's dialogue strengthens its realism.

But such patterns are also observable at the individual level. Maybe all your friends use the same language and speech patterns. But you probably know a few people who have distinct ways of speaking. Most of us have certain words that we often use or particular ways of stringing words together that differ slightly from our friends and family. Maybe you know someone who says *dude* a lot or who pauses at unusual intervals. Dialogue that is styled in a way that is unique to each character can lend realism and believability to the characters, and the more realistic the characters are, the more likely it is that audiences will attach to them.

There are two ways to depict characters' thoughts, either by using exposition to tell readers what the characters are thinking or through thought dialogue:

Exposition: she didn't think the house was big enough.
Thought dialogue: *the house isn't big enough,* she thought.

Sharing the characters' thoughts helps readers get to know and understand the characters better. Thoughts are often used to reveal necessary information about the story. As with regular dialogue, thought dialogue often carries a flavor or tone that is particular to each character, adding to their realism.

Dialogue is also an important tool for revealing the characters' backstories and the history of the story world. Although some stories will use information dumps and flashbacks, characters can also talk about the past. For example, one character might say to another, "Remember when...?" This is a useful method of filling in the blanks regarding what occurred before the story's starting point, as long as it fits naturally in the conversation and doesn't feel forced.

Dialogue is used to move a story forward in many ways,

from establishing the characters' personalities to developing relationships between the characters.

Action and Dialogue Working Together

Action and dialogue serve a story best when they work together and are interspersed in a smooth way. Characters do things while they talk. They eat, they pace, they make faces and gestures, they use body language. And characters talk while they do things. They chat while eating, working, and traveling.

Although some stories are successful with long sequences of dialogue that don't include much action, scenes tend to come alive better in readers' minds when chatter is interspersed with action. But as with all elements of storytelling, both the action and the dialogue should be necessary to the story and should move it forward in meaningful ways.

Action and dialogue can also be used to reveal important information about a story that would otherwise have to be explained through description or exposition. Description is an important part of storytelling because it helps readers visualize the story world. However, the world can be revealed through characters' actions and dialogues. For example, instead of using narrative to describe a room when the characters enter, the characters can physically interact with it and talk about it. This sets the scene without dragging readers through lengthy paragraphs of description.

It may be possible to write an entire story that is all dialogue and no action, but it better be excellent and gripping dialogue. Likewise, a story could be all action and no dialogue, but again, that action will need to be pretty special to keep audiences tuned in. Strong and balanced action and dialogue that work together to show readers what's happening in a story is most effective.

8

Description, Exposition, and Transition

Description and exposition work together to help audiences visualize a story while transition helps us move between scenes.

Description

Without description, readers wouldn't be able to visualize what's happening in a story. We need to see the setting and the characters. Because there are no visuals in prose, writers must use words to describe a story's visual elements in a way that helps readers see the story playing out in their minds.

Prior to film and photography, prose was packed with lengthy and detailed description. If a story was set on a tropical island, the narrative needed to describe it in great detail, because most readers had no idea what a tropical island looked like. Nowadays, most people have some idea of what a tropical island looks like, thanks to films and photos, and many people have traveled to a tropical island, thanks to advances in transportation. This lessens the need for elaborate descriptions. Modern writers can therefore write simpler and more concise descriptions, which allows them to place greater emphasis on action and dialogue. This is a good thing, because action and dialogue are where a story really happens.

Description is most essential when we're describing

characters, locations, and objects that readers have never seen or experienced. These can be some of the trickiest types of descriptions to craft. In a science-fiction story, it can be challenging to describe an alien to an audience that has never seen such a creature. We can use points of reference: maybe the alien is humanoid in shape, maybe it has some features that we can compare to plants and animals on Earth. But tying it all together in a tidy description that truly matches what the author is imagining might be a formidable task. Word choice and sentence structure are critical to clear and vivid descriptions that are interesting or exciting.

Let's consider a description of a room. There is a bookshelf in one corner and a chair in the opposite corner. There's a couch and a coffee table in the center of the room. A piano sits in front of a large picture window. The walls are wood paneled and covered with paintings.

This description may give you a sense of the room, but it's boring. Readers are likely to drift off if a description continues like this for too long.

What's wrong with this description? Almost every sentence begins with "There is" or some variation of it, and most of the verbs are various forms of *to be*. Although it's useful to draft descriptions in this manner, these sentences need to be reworked so that they hold the reader's attention:

> A massive oak desk sat below a large picture window, beside a shelf overflowing with books. Hardcovers, paperbacks, and binders were piled on the tiled floor in messy stacks.

Note the use of active verbs, such as *overflowing*, and

descriptive adjectives, like *dingy*. Good narrative description makes the setting more vivid by using language that engages the reader.

Effective description is often achieved not by inserting long and specific descriptions but by making thoughtful decisions about what to include and what to leave out. When a narrative brings readers into a room, it doesn't need to cite every object in the room and explain in minute detail how the room is laid out. The goal is to give readers a sense of the room. That is best achieved by providing readers just enough description that they can see key details and trusting that their imaginations will fill in the rest.

Description also determines how immersed readers get in the story. We could describe the sand on a beach as white and sprawling in every direction as far as the eye could see. But if the character is walking on the sand, the reader will become more immersed when the sand is hot, grainy, and gritty against the character's feet. When description is visceral—when we can feel it—it comes alive.

Description can be used to trigger readers' five senses: sight, sound, smell, touch, and taste. Average descriptions focus on sight, explaining what something looks like. But descriptions that include the other senses will arouse the readers' senses. This is why dining scenes work remarkably well in prose. We can use description to set a scene in which characters are cooking a meal: the warmth from the oven; bright, fresh vegetables steaming on the stove; the sound of a sizzling skillet; the smell of spiced chicken frying; the sound of an ice-cold bottle of beer cracking open. The readers' mouths will water as the characters enjoy their spicy, zesty fajitas.

The most important descriptions are those that are essential to the story. Have you ever read a story that offered detailed descriptions of mundane items and locations and then skimmed over the descriptive details of story elements that really mattered? This causes readers to struggle to imagine the story. For example, if a character has been in a terrible accident and is getting bandages removed for the first time, there should be some description of the wounds or scars as opposed to a description of the hospital room. This helps the readers focus on the character (and therefore the story) as opposed to a generic room. By adding description that references the smell of antiseptic and the slick, cold texture of the doctor's latex gloves, the scene becomes sensory and visceral.

One of the tricks for writing good description deals with placement. Many novice writers have a tendency to pause a story in order to describe things when they first appear. For example, every time a new character appears, there's a paragraph of description. Sometimes all description in a story is organized in this manner—set apart from the action and dialogue. In other cases, the description of a character may occur after we've been with the character through several chapters. It's awkward to spend hours with a character and then find out she has flaming red hair. By that time, readers have already plugged in their own image of the character and may be seeing the character with black, brown, or blond hair.

Although descriptive paragraphs are often necessary, description is richest when it's intertwined with action and dialogue. Characters can brush their red hair out of their eyes, rub their tired blue eyes, shrug out of their tattered old gray hoodies. Instead of pausing to describe a character, we can see her through another character's eyes. Maybe one character sees another character's hair and says, "I haven't seen hair that color red since my best friend from childhood moved away when we were six years old." Now we've learned one character's hair color and also learned something about the other character's childhood. Action can reveal description by showing characters interacting with their environment. Instead of describing a character's jacket, we see the character putting it on, rolling up the sleeves, or spilling something on it: *she pulled on her brown corduroy blazer and noticed a stain on the cuff.*

It won't always be possible to place description in action and dialogue. Blocked description that occupies several consecutive sentences, paragraphs, or pages is useful when describing a new world or some item that the reader is not familiar with. However, using active and compelling language makes long excerpts of description easier for readers to digest.

Exposition

Writers often talk about the need to show instead of tell. Don't tell us the character disarmed a bomb; show the character sweating over the fuse as the timer counts down to zero. We want to see it!

However, there are many parts of a story that must be told instead of shown. This is called exposition. It's how stories relay important background information and details that cannot or should not be shown.

For example, in a mystery story written in first person, we may get something like the following:

I've been at this for twenty years, and I've put away a lot of scumbags. Got in a lot of scrapes with gnarly suspects. Been shot twice. Did countless stints in the ER with cuts, scrapes, bruises, and broken bones.

This part of the narrative is setting up the story world and establishing the character. There isn't time or space in a novel to show us the entirety of the characters' experiences, so we summarize, reveal, and explain through exposition. There is no action or dialogue in exposition; nothing is happening onscreen, but we're learning important story details because the narrative is telling us what we need to know.

One of the most common forms of exposition is backstory, the events that occurred before the story. A narrative may include a paragraph of backstory so that we understand something significant about the character or setting. For example, a paragraph of exposition might tell us that a character has spent the past three months training for a marathon. This may be important information that the reader doesn't need to see happening onscreen but needs to know about. Backstory exposition is often used to convey key details about characters' pasts, such as events from their childhoods. These details should be relevant—even essential—to the story proper.

Some stories contain a lot of exposition, pages upon pages of it. While readers connect more with action and dialogue, truly intriguing exposition can be just as riveting, especially if it's necessary to the story at hand and well crafted. *The Girl with the Dragon Tattoo* is an example of a highly successful novel that was made into two different films and that is packed with lengthy exposition that gives readers a deeper understanding of the story.

Transition

The simplest definition of *transition* is "change." In storytelling, transitions are the changes that move through time, to new locations, or to different points of view. Transitions also carry us into new scenes and chapters.

Effective transitions are smooth; the change registers in readers' minds but they don't notice it. Weak transitions are muddled or jarring; they confuse readers or yank them out of the story, causing a negative reading experience. If you've ever read a story and found yourself lost in time, confused about the location of a scene, or unsure of which character's perspective you were reading, you've likely experienced a poor transition.

Exposition is sometimes used ineffectively as a transition. If something important happens to a character in the morning and the next important moment is in the evening, the story needs to traverse the afternoon. However, readers don't need to be taken on an expository tour through every minute of the character's day. We don't need to see them sitting at their desk, staring at a computer screen, thinking about what to have for dinner, and so on. A transition should be used to move from the morning to the evening in a few short words.

Similarly, when the characters are moving between locations, we don't need to see them getting into their cars. We don't need to know who's riding with whom or which route they're taking. Transitions can be used to let the reader know the story has moved to a new location, allowing the story to jump from point A to point B quickly and seamlessly.

There may be a good reason to take the reader through the character's afternoon, and sometimes the ride between locations should be included. But they should be included because what's happening is relevant to the story, not because the story needs a bridge to move from one point in time and space to another.

Fortunately, there are plenty of tools that writers can use to craft transitions, the most obvious being chapter breaks and scene breaks. Some scene and chapter breaks include transitional markers. For example, a chapter heading might include the time or place where the events of the chapter occur: Chapter 12: New Orleans, 1972.

While scene and chapter breaks don't always indicate a change in time or location, readers understand them as a signal that a change of some kind is occurring. If it's not a change in time or space, then it's probably a dramatic change in the story or a shift to a different point of view.

Although chapter and scene breaks provide good transitional signals, a new scene or chapter needs to establish the new time, place, and character perspective. This is best done early on so that readers can get their bearings before getting into the new scene or chapter.

Time jumps often use transitional phrases, such as *three months later* or *the next day.* Similarly, locations can be indicated with transitional phrases. For example, a scene might start as follows: *the bitter cold of the Alaskan winter hit me like a thousand knives when I stepped off the plane.* If the previous scene was in New York, the reader will know the location has moved to Alaska.

In the series *A Song of Ice and Fire*, George R. R. Martin

uses numerous point-of-view characters. Each chapter includes a heading that lets readers know which character's point of view is used for the chapter. This is the simplest and most effective way to transition between points of view.

The key to an effective transition is to make it clear to the reader that something has changed, whether it's the time, place, or point of view. Scene and chapter breaks are good ways to transition, but regardless of whether breaks are used, transitions should be marked by clear signals within the narrative that let readers know a change has occurred. These transitions should clearly establish the new time, location, or point of view.

9

Chapters, Scenes, and Sequences

Chapters, scenes, and sequences are structural units of storytelling. These are the basic blocks of a story that contain all other elements, from characters, plot, and setting to action, dialogue, and description.

Chapters

Chapters are units within a book that are named, numbered, or both. Chapters provide numerous functions: they break a story into digestible components; they provide transitions between moments in time, locations, or points of view; and they provide a novel with structure.

There are no rules regarding chapter length. Some chapters are short; others are long. Some novels contain chapters that are all roughly the same length; others contain chapters that vary in length. The length of a story's chapters is driven by the story and the author's judgment. However, chapter length should be comfortable and flow with the story's pacing.

Similarly, there are no rules regarding when to start or end a chapter. Some chapters end on cliffhangers, which keep readers turning the pages. Some chapters wrap up neatly, providing pauses within a story.

A chapter can be comprised of a single scene, but it can also contain multiple scenes.

Scenes

According to the *Oxford Dictionary*, a scene is "a sequence of continuous action in a play, film, opera, or book." Each scene usually occurs in a single location: in one scene, the characters are sitting in a bar having a conversation. In the next scene, a character is getting into a taxicab.

We have developed shorthand to refer to certain types of scenes that often appear in stories: love scenes, action scenes, and fight scenes are a few examples. A scene that takes us into a character's dream might be a single scene, but it's usually called a dream sequence. Other common types of scenes drop the word *scene* altogether. We don't normally refer to a "car chase sequence." We just refer to the "car chase." Also, the first scene is always called the opening scene while the final scene in a story is called the closing scene.

The setting of each scene should be clear from its onset. Readers struggle with narrative when they're not sure where or when a scene is taking place. Simple markers that communicate the time, place, and point of view help readers identify the setting and perspective of a scene.

Each scene is a miniature story within the story and has a beginning, middle, and end. A scene opens, there's conflict, and then the scene closes. At the scene level, conflict is usually minor; the larger story conflict is spread throughout the entire story.

Some storytellers say that each scene should contain an emotional transition, which can help build tension into a scene and gives the story emotional flow. If a scene starts on a positive note (the protagonist is happy), then it can end on a negative note (the protagonist is sad). These emotional or tonal shifts don't need to be intense or dramatic. Something as simple as showing a clumsy character spilling wine all over his white shirt can give a scene a downward emotional shift.

However, these emotional shifts are not required—and in fact, they're not always possible. Some stories require a series of scenes that maintain a constant tone without significant emotional shifts.

The core function of any scene is to move the story forward with plot and character development. The more development a scene contains, the richer it becomes. One scene can move the plot forward while another scene develops the protagonist, but if the plot and character development can be contained within a single scene (rather than two separate scenes), then that scene will be more powerful.

Although chapters and sequences are important structural units, scenes are a story's most essential and basic units. On a smaller scale, scenes must do what the larger story is doing: reveal the characters, unfold the plot, establish the setting, and explore the theme.

Sequences

A sequence is a series of scenes that form a single narrative unit. A sequence can be defined in several ways: by the timeline (for example, showing what three different characters are doing in different locations at the same time). It could be defined by a single location (what happens in a particular location over time). However, a sequence can show multiple times and locations. Sequences are most easily identified as a series of scenes that are closely linked.

A battle sequence could be comprised of scenes that show an entire battle from beginning to end: warriors prepare for battle by donning armor and wielding weapons. They travel to a battlefield. Multiple scenes show the fighting, as we see various characters combating the enemy. And the final scene in such a sequence would show the aftermath of the battle.

Although a sequence can move through space and time, there's a central event occurring that ties the scenes within it together.

10

Literary Devices and Narrative Techniques

Writers use literary devices to convey or illustrate thoughts, ideas, and images or to strengthen their prose. Narrative techniques are a subset of literary devices that are specifically used in narrative writing. Both literary devices and narrative techniques occur naturally in writing but are also used intentionally. Learning about the many literary devices and narrative techniques that are available will add weight to your writer's toolbox.

Literary Devices

One of the most popular literary devices is the metaphor, which is when we refer to one thing as something else. For example: she is a ray of sunshine. Metaphors should not be confused with similes, which refer to one thing as being *like* something else: she is like a ray of sunshine.

Among the wide range of literary devices, some particular to certain forms of writing. For example, a poetic device is a type of literary device that is only (or mostly) used in poetry. But many literary devices can be applied to any form of writing.

Literary devices that enrich the prose help writers make the best possible choices with language, resulting in a more pleasurable experience for readers. One such example is alliteration. This is the practice of repeating a consonant sound two or more times in close proximity. It's most commonly done with two words with the consonant sound occurring at the beginning of both words; the T sound in *tick tock* is an example of alliteration. However, alliteration can be buried within a single word, which is exemplified by the B sound in the word *blueberry*, or it can be even more sporadic, as with the B sound in *big robot*. This repetition of sound adds cadence or rhythm to the writing, giving it a musical quality.

Alliteration is just one of many literary devices that are available to writers who want to craft rich prose. If you feel a sentence or paragraph is monotonous or droning, a literary device might provide a way to spice it up by looking at the language with an eye for making it more compelling.

Poets tend to focus on language more than other writers, as a large part of poetic artistry is concerned with these elements of the craft. One of the best ways to master literary devices that enrich prose is to read poetry and learn to identify literary devices within poems and other forms of writing. Writing poetry and incorporating literary devices is also a good way to cement your understanding of them. If you set out to write a poem that contains one metaphor, one simile, and two instances of alliteration, then you can quickly and easily work with these devices and see how they benefit the language.

Narrative Techniques

As useful as literary devices are, most storytellers are more interested in narrative techniques. A narrative technique is a specific kind of literary device that is used in storytelling. Some narrative techniques are widely used and can be found in most stories, while others are common in certain genres. And some are best avoided. Narrative techniques should be used selectively, depending on what the story needs.

One of the most widely used narrative techniques is the inciting incident. This is a moment in a story where things change for the protagonist, marking the moment when the central conflict launches into action. In the *Harry Potter* series, it's when Harry receives his first owl post inviting him to Hogwarts. In *The Hunger Games*, it's when Katniss's sister is selected as a tribute and Katniss volunteers in her place. The inciting incident is the moment when the Hero's Journey truly begins, when the story kicks off after the setup has been established. It's difficult to find a story that doesn't contain an inciting incident.

A variety of narrative techniques are staples of genres. For example, a red herring is a literary technique used mostly in mystery stories. Readers are encouraged to solve the story's mystery or puzzle, and a red herring is a clue that leads the audience in the wrong direction. Sometimes there are multiple red herrings that lead readers' suspicions away from the true culprit.

There are also narrative techniques that can help storytellers avoid poor storytelling. These are techniques that may be used effectively on rare occasions but are usually hallmarks of weak plot points and amateur storytelling. Deus ex machina is a narrative technique in which characters are saved from a hopeless situation by a surprise character or unlikely event. Deus ex machina often pulls from the supernatural, such as when a god or magical creature saves a character, especially when this supernatural being has never been mentioned before in the story. In *The Lord of the Rings*, a Great Eagle conveniently shows up and rescues Frodo when he's trapped on Mount Doom. In the *Harry Potter* series, a phoenix rescues Harry by bringing him a sword that was conveniently hidden in a hat. Both of these are examples of deus ex machina: the characters are trapped with no way out, and a surprising, somewhat unbelievable, and often super-powered entity shows up out of the blue to save the day. Because deus ex machina often feels too convenient and lacks believability, it's best avoided if possible.

Narrative techniques are useful to writers in several ways, including troubleshooting. Some of the most common narrative techniques, like the inciting incident, function as milestones in almost every story. Authors can use these milestones to make sure their stories are on track. If the inciting incident occurs at the halfway mark of the story, an author knows there's a problem and the story needs work, because inciting incidents should occur near the beginning. After all, it's what kicks off the story.

Literary devices and narrative techniques are so common that many are inherent to storytelling. Novice storytellers may not even know that a story beat they've devised is actually a recognized narrative technique.

Anyone who wants to master the art of storytelling would be well served by studying narrative techniques and adding these tools to their toolboxes, as they are highly useful for every aspect of storytelling from devising a basic plot to polishing the finer points of the language. To start learning more, check the appendix, where you'll find a glossary that includes a litany of literary devices and narrative techniques.

Part Three: Structure

11

Concept, Premise, and Logline

Most audiences are first introduced to stories as concepts, premises, or loglines. These are hooks used for pitching and marketing; they draw people's attention, get them interested in a story, and compel them to buy it.

Writers often start with a concept or premise as the initial idea for a story. It's certainly not the only way for a story to be born, but identifying a clear concept or premise early on can lend clarity as you work your way through the composition of a story.

People often confuse the words *concept* and *premise* and use them interchangeably, but they have different meanings, which are important for storytellers to understand.

Concept

Concept tells us what a story is about—the core idea of a story. There are two types of concepts: low concepts and high concepts.

Low Concepts

Low concepts are simple and can come off as generic or mundane at first glance. However, these stories often contain more character development and nuance than their high-concept counterparts.

Low concepts don't have built-in conflicts and

antagonists. Nor do they appear on their surfaces to be particularly unique or compelling. They are more difficult to pitch or sell because they're harder for audiences to envision. However, if well executed, low-concept stories can perform well.

Here are some examples of low concepts: two teenagers fall in love; a widow struggles with grief; a detective solves a crime.

Teenagers fall in love every day. What's so interesting about that? This is what makes low concept a harder sell; it often needs to be worked into a fuller premise to hold any real interest.

High Concepts

High concepts pack a lot of punch in just a few words. They often wrestle with what-if questions and tend to contain built-in appeal while conveying a fresh or original idea—or a new twist on an old idea. Many high concepts focus on primal emotions and situations, such as survival or finding love. The conflict and genre are often self-evident. These concepts are visual; in just a few words, they spark people's imaginations. A one-line description is enough to draw people's attention:

- What if scientists built dinosaurs from preserved DNA? (*Jurassic Park*)

- A lonely orphan is invited to a secret school for young wizards. (*Harry Potter*)

- What happens when artificial intelligence surpasses human intelligence? (*The Terminator, The Matrix, Battlestar Galactica*)

As you can see, these are all genre stories, which isn't unusual; science fiction and fantasy lend themselves particularly well to high concepts.

Premise

Concepts are often too broad and are only interesting on the surface—even high concepts. A hundred storytellers could start with the same concept—high or low—and they'll end up with a hundred different premises. For example, you could take the idea of genetically engineered dinosaurs in many different directions. The dinosaurs could be built in a lab and then escape and wreak havoc on a metropolitan population. Their DNA could be mixed with human DNA, resulting in a highly intelligent species that wants to wipe out its main competitor—humans. And the dinosaurs don't have to be antagonistic: they could help humans solve a serious problem. Maybe they can communicate with the aliens that have just arrived. Now we're heading toward something that resembles a premise.

A concept is an idea for a story, whereas a premise is a very brief sketch of a story. Concept gives us a general idea of what a story is about—a view from afar. Premise pulls the camera in closer so that we get a better sense of what's going on in this story.

A premise introduces character, plot, and possibly setting. It gives us a sense of the obstacles the characters will face. It goes into specifics:

- Scientists build dinosaurs from preserved DNA and then fight them off when they threaten to take over a theme park that is under construction. (*Jurassic Park*)

- A lonely orphan is invited to a secret school for young wizards, where he will eventually acquire the skills and allies he needs to face the evil and powerful wizard who killed his parents. (*Harry Potter*)

- Two teenagers from rival families fall in love and make the ultimate sacrifice for each other. (*Romeo and Juliet*)

The premise for *Romeo and Juliet* shows how a low concept (two teenagers fall in love) can be turned into a more compelling premise with a little tweaking.

As you can see, a premise expands on a concept, making it more interesting by adding details about the story's world or conflict. A premise reveals details about the protagonist, provides the story's setup, and identifies the antagonist and the core conflict.

Logline

Loglines tend to be used more for movies than for novels, but we're seeing increasing usage among authors and publishers who need short and pithy descriptions of their books, especially for online advertising.

A logline is a one- or two-sentence description of your story, similar to an elevator pitch, which is when you summarize your product or service in the amount of time it takes to ride an elevator, about thirty seconds. With a logline, you've got a maximum of two sentences to pitch your story. You can use your logline when talking to agents, editors, and readers. In fact, a polished logline is a good way to test your story idea and see how people respond to it.

Loglines usually include the following elements: the protagonist, the antagonist, and a hook that summarizes the plot. The concept and the premise are all wrapped up in a good, strong logline that makes your story appealing to prospects without giving away any spoilers.

Check out the logline for the 1997 film *Titanic*: "A seventeen-year-old aristocrat falls in love with a kind, but poor artist aboard the luxurious, ill-fated R.M.S. Titanic."

Let's take a closer look at this logline.

You'll notice that the protagonist is clearly identified as a "seventeen-year-old aristocrat." The logline gives us one adjective (seventeen-year-old) and one noun (aristocrat). Note that *aristocrat* is a very specific and precise noun (as opposed to *girl*, *woman*, or *teenager*).

The protagonist's love interest is described as a "kind, but poor artist." Again, the noun is specific. He's not a man or a boy; he's an artist. And here we get two adjectives. He's "kind, but poor." The fact that he's poor contrasted against her being an aristocrat is what matters here; there's built-in relationship tension when we bring together people from different worlds—in this case, from different classes. Finally, we come to the antagonist, which in this case is not a character. The antagonist is the *Titanic* itself, the notoriously "ill-fated" ship that sank in 1912. Of course, the ship is not the only antagonist in the film. Rose's fiancé serves as the story's villain. However, the logline needs to entice the audience. The famous ship that hit an iceberg and sank will automatically generate more interest than some unknown fiancé.

In reading the logline, we learn a lot about the story. A rich girl falls in love with a poor artist aboard a historical sinking ship. That's a lot of information from just a single sentence.

Put simply, a logline is designed to spark interest in the story and compel people to buy, read, or watch it. If you can come up with a good logline for your story, you'll have a much easier time selling it.

Using Concept, Premise, and Logline for Story Development

Concept and premise are useful tools for storytellers throughout the creative process. The initial seed of a story may very well be its concept. However, if a story's inception comes from some other source of inspiration, such as a character or setting, then turning it into a concept will often give a storyteller some much-needed direction.

Let's say you want to write a story about artificial intelligence—super-smart robots. That's a good start, but it's not quite a concept. Developing that idea into a concept will make it more concrete: *super-intelligent robots gain access to nuclear weapons.*

We can take it a step further by expanding this concept into a premise, which will bring more clarity to the idea: *a programmer who built the world's first super-intelligent robots races to stop them from gaining access to nuclear weapons.*

Because loglines are primarily used to market books and movies, it may seem like you should write your logline after your book is completed. However, writing your logline in advance has several benefits: identifying key features of the protagonist and antagonist will shape your character development, and figuring out the central conflict will give your story focus. Establishing these elements before you write a draft can result in a tighter story that requires fewer revisions. Can you turn the concept about super-intelligent robots into a compelling logline?

Concepts, premises, and loglines come in handy whether you're writing, pitching, or selling a story. Agents and editors respond well to compelling concepts and premises, and audiences respond to them too. As you tell people you're working on a novel, many will ask, "What's it about?" That's a question that might tie your tongue in knots, but if you've prepared and polished your logline, you'll be ready with an intriguing answer, and you can use it to test your story idea on people to see what kind of reactions it gets.

12

Story Structure

Structure is a story's framework. It determines what happens onscreen, the interweaving of every element within a story. We take all the building blocks—character, plot, setting, and theme—and then we get out our hammer and nails and build them into a framework.

Structure can refer to classic story frameworks, such as the three-act structure or the Hero's Journey. These are universal story structures with common storytelling patterns. However, we can also use the term *structure* to refer to the structure of a particular story that we are studying, analyzing, or developing.

There are no rules for building a story structure. Some writers start with an outline, which is often based on a classic structure. Others start writing without any planning, but a structure emerges as the draft evolves.

For many writers, developing a structure is an exciting step in the writing process, because it's where we start to see a story take shape.

Structural Formulas

The terms *plot*, *structure*, and *formula* are often used interchangeably. Although they are closely related and sometimes indistinguishable, these terms have different meanings. A plot refers to the events that occur in a story. Structure refers to the order and pacing of the events.

Formula is a preestablished series of beats that are used to craft a story.

Consider the following story structure: we meet the main characters, get to know them, and find out what they want and what's preventing them from achieving their goals. Then there's an inciting incident that shakes things up and launches the characters into some kind of adventure.

Story formulas get a bad rap because they can cause stories to feel generic and...well...formulaic. Audiences don't respond well to stories that they feel they've read a thousand times before. And among storytellers, writers who use formulas are sometimes criticized for lacking originality.

However, formulas can be used as guiding principles to ensure that a story progresses in a way that is emotionally or intellectually satisfying. And because we can see the structure of some formulas in countless beloved stories, the structures themselves can be viewed as universal patterns that occur in storytelling.

There are countless models that we can use to formulate a story. Some models are simple, such as the three-act structure. Others are far more complex and delve into specific plot points, like the Hero's Journey. Writing advisers often use these structures to teach storytelling, and many authors, editors, and other industry leaders have come up with formulas of their own.

Joseph Campbell was a mythologist who discovered one such pattern, which he called the Monomyth (or Hero's Journey). Campbell identified a storytelling pattern in numerous myths, legends, and other stories throughout history and across cultures. He surmised that the pattern was a universal reflection of something within human consciousness. The Monomyth wasn't a formula that storytellers used with intention; it occurred naturally, demonstrating that established story structures have widespread and deep psychological appeal.

The three-act structure is the most widely used structure in the world. Elegant in its simplicity of three acts, which include setup, conflict, and resolution, the three-act structure ensures that a story has a beginning, middle, and end while leaving plenty of room for an author to be creative.

We'll look more closely at the three-act structure and the Hero's Journey in the next chapter.

Stories tend to feel formulaic when they are forced into a predesigned template, whereas stories that follow a familiar structural pattern feel comfortable and familiar, even if they are packed with surprises. They key to using structures and formulas effectively is to be flexible and deviate from the formula when necessary.

Ultimately, each writer needs to find the process that works for them. That may mean working within structural guidelines, or it may mean working more freely. However, there are plenty of benefits that come from working within an established structure, even a loose one. These structures provide a road map for a story, keep the plot and characters focused, and almost always make the writing process much faster.

13

The Three-Act Structure and the Hero's Journey

Two of the most widely used story structures, which writers use to develop and formulate stories as well as analyze them, are the three-act structure and the Hero's Journey. Let's take an in-depth look at both. See if you can identify these patterns in stories you've enjoyed.

The Three-Act Structure

The most common story structure (some even argue it's a necessary structure) is the three-act structure. It's widely used by storytellers in every medium from short stories to video games. For something so simple, it's been analyzed, deconstructed, picked apart, and rebuilt by plenty of story scholars. But at its most basic, the three-act structure goes like this:

Act I: Setup
Act II: Conflict
Act III: Resolution

Like I said, it's simple. But there are many takes on the three-act structure. Some versions of the Hero's Journey, which we'll examine next, designate where each act should begin and end within a larger and more complex structure. In screenwriting, many experts say that act one should be 25 percent of the story, act two should be 50 percent, and act three should be the final 25 percent. Screenwriting guru Blake Snyder even renamed the acts, calling them thesis, antithesis, and synthesis.

The structure of three acts serves an important purpose, especially for beginning storytellers, which is to remind them of the three major movements that are universally found in stories: the beginning, the middle, and the end. It can be helpful to look at your outline or draft and ask where the shift into each act occurs. If these shifts are unclear or if the acts don't provide setup, conflict, and resolution, respectively, then there may be some major wrinkles that need to be ironed out.

The three-act structure is so basic that it begs to be made more complicated and elaborate. Keeping in mind that, at its most basic, it's nothing more than setup, conflict, and resolution, let's take a look at some of the common story beats we see in each act.

Act I: Setup

The first act introduces us to the characters, their relationships, and the story world. We meet the protagonist and find out what their goal is and what's holding them back from achieving it. The protagonist is faced with a conflict. Dealing with this conflict leads to a second and more dramatic conflict, which is the inciting incident. The inciting incident can be an opportunity (positive) or a challenge (negative); it imposes a dramatic and permanent change for the protagonist, and it raises the central story question or challenge.

Act II: Conflict

The second act is the middle of the story, which is filled with rising action, as the stakes get higher and the tension increases. Throughout this act, the protagonist attempts to tackle the challenge or solve the problem at the heart of the story. Usually, these attempts only cause the situation to worsen. Along the way, there are successes and failures, so the rising action isn't a smooth rise to the top; rather, it's jagged but trending upward (or downward). Often, failure occurs because the protagonist does not possess the skills or traits necessary to achieve the goal. Therefore, a key element of the second act shows the protagonist acquiring the skills or traits needed to meet the challenge they face. These can be material skills or an adjustment to the character's attitude, behavior, or beliefs; this is the central character arc working itself out. It's during this act that the antagonist presents a series of obstacles for the protagonist, and often friends and sidekicks provide the protagonist with assistance.

Act III: Resolution

The third act is when the story problem and all subplots get resolved. Its most noteworthy feature is the climax, which is the most intense moment of the story when conflict, tension, and stakes are at their highest. It's the final battle (not necessarily a literal battle; in fact, it can be an internal battle). The story question gets answered once and for all, leaving the protagonist, and often the other main characters and even the story world, dramatically changed from what they were in the beginning.

Although the vast majority of stories use a three-act

structure, there are four- and five-act structures as well.

Four- and Five-Act Structures

The four-act structure splits the second act into two separate acts. Act one is setup. Act two shows the protagonist trying to solve the problem but failing. In act three, the protagonist recovers and comes up with a new plan, but all is lost. Act four introduces a new plan that works, and the protagonist emerges victorious.

The five-act structure starts with act one, a prologue that sets up the story by introducing the characters, story world, and central conflict. Act two features rising action. Act three features the climax or turning point. Act four is based on falling action as the story approaches the end and all plot threads are tied up. Act five is the denouement or final outcome.

The Hero's Journey

Mythologist Joseph Campbell discovered recurrent patterns in myths, legends, and folklore. These patterns occurred in stories throughout human history and all around the globe. He recorded these observations in a book called *The Hero with a Thousand Faces*. This is the book that gave us the Monomyth, which is more commonly known as the Hero's Journey.

This pattern was most famously adopted by George Lucas, and the Monomyth's influence can be seen clearly in the epic *Star Wars* films. In fact, the original *Star Wars* trilogy is often used to teach the Hero's Journey and storytelling, and George Lucas has cited Joseph Campbell as one of his mentors.

Although it was brilliant, Campbell's work was dense, highly academic, and spent a lot of time on the connection between psychology and mythology (as well as stories from religious traditions). It identified common patterns in storytelling, but it focused on myths, legends, and folklore, leaving out other genres. It was also rooted deep in the past, because it was based mostly on ancient tales. Human culture has since evolved, and so has storytelling.

Enter Christopher Vogler, a Hollywood script analyst with a keen eye for compelling stories. He studied Campbell's work and produced a seven-page memo for his peers to help them improve the stories they were developing. Vogler had reworked Campbell's discoveries into a simple model for storytellers—a model that was applicable to all stories, not just myths and ancient legends. The memo became legendary in the storytelling world and was eventually expanded into a book called *The Writer's Journey*, which I consider to be the seminal book on storytelling.

Storytellers have developed several variations on the Hero's Journey. It's a structure worth studying, as it can be found in a high percentage of popular stories from *The Lord of the Rings* series to *The Hunger Games* trilogy. When executed well, the Hero's Journey resonates with audiences on a deep, psychological level.

The Hero's Journey is so universal that storytellers may inadvertently follow some or all of its stages in the stories they write, even without studying the structure formally. But many writers also use it with intention, as a guide. As a narrative tool, it provides valuable insight that every storyteller should examine.

Examples of some famous films that follow the Hero's Journey include *The Wizard of Oz*, *Star Wars*, *The Matrix*, *Harry Potter*, and *Titanic*. Searching YouTube for the Hero's Journey will bring up dozens of videos that show how the Hero's Journey is executed in these and other movies, but nothing delves into the Hero's Journey quite as accurately or insightfully as Vogler's book.

Vogler's shorter version of the Hero's Journey condensed Campbell's structure into twelve, rather than seventeen, stages and added the Ordinary World, which is a key component of setting up a story. It's also gender neutral and uses updated language. This structure is highly common in modern films and literature. It could be considered the core version of the Hero's Journey with the additional stages and details in Campbell's version being useful for adding extra depth and historical, mythological elements.

Because Vogler's version is more universal, we'll examine it here. However, reading Campbell's work is recommended, as it will provide a much deeper and thorough understanding of the model.

The Hero's Journey consists of eight archetypes and twelve story stages. After the description of each archetype and stage, you'll find the corresponding example from *Star Wars: Episode IV – A New Hope*, which includes spoilers, in case you haven't seen the film.

The Eight Archetypes of the Hero's Journey

The Hero's Journey starts with eight archetypes. They are often characters, but archetypes are better viewed as functions or energies in a story. Each of these archetypes has a very specific job to do within the story. Some characters may perform the functions of multiple archetypes, and events or objects may fulfill some archetypal roles (such as when a book provides the function of a mentor).

- **Hero:** protagonist who undergoes a meaningful transformation through the story. Luke Skywalker.

- **Herald:** signals that an adventure (or change) is imminent. R2-D2.

- **Mentor:** teacher and guide. Obi-Wan Kenobi.

- **Threshold Guardian:** guards who block a threshold, which the Hero must pass. Stormtroopers at Mos Eisley.

- **Shadow:** the villain and other characters who stand in the Hero's way; they often embody the Hero's negative or undesirable traits. Darth Vader, stormtroopers.

- **Shapeshifter:** a character or entity whose motives or intentions are unclear. Han Solo.

- **Trickster:** comic relief; Tricksters are often catalysts for change. R2-D2, C-3PO.

- **Allies:** the Hero's friends and helpers. Han, Leia.

The Twelve Stages of the Hero's Journey

The Hero's Journey then delves into twelve stages of a story. This is not an outline or a formula. The stages can occur out of order, and they can overlap one another. This is a very loose guide that we can use to assess a story's structure and identify its core beats.

ACT I

1. **Ordinary World** We meet the Hero, and we're introduced to his or her world. Luke Skywalker is a bored orphan, living with his aunt and uncle on a moisture farm; he wants to leave the farm and go to the pilot academy.

2. **Call to Adventure.** Something (usually a Herald) signals that change is afoot. R2-D2 plays an intriguing holographic message showing a pretty woman saying, "Help me, Obi-Wan Kenobi. You're my only hope."

3. **Refusal of the Call.** The Hero refuses to answer the Call to Adventure, often citing excuses. Luke Skywalker insists he can't accompany Obi-Wan Kenobi because he must stay and help his uncle on the farm.

4. **Meeting with the Mentor.** The Hero encounters a Mentor, who will provide guidance and bestow necessary tools and skills. Obi-Wan gives Luke a lightsaber that belonged to Luke's father and trains him to use the Force.

5. **Crossing the First Threshold.** The Hero passes the First Threshold, leaving the Ordinary World and entering the Special World of the story. Obi-Wan and Luke go to Mos Eisley, a smarmy town, where they must get past stormtroopers and other nefarious characters, eventually getting off the planet Tatooine altogether.

ACT II

6. **Tests, Allies, and Enemies.** The Hero acquires allies (often building a team), faces tests, and establishes enemies. Luke acquires helpers, such as Han and Leia. Darth Vader becomes his enemy when Vader strikes Obi-Wan down. Luke and his friends face numerous tests in their journey from Tatooine to the Death Star. In Star Wars, this stage of the journey stretches from the end of the act one through the end of act two, overlapping several other stages.

7. **Approach to the Inmost Cave.** The Hero (usually accompanied by Allies) approaches the story's central Ordeal. The Millennium Falcon is sucked into the Death Star.

8. **Ordeal.** The Ordeal often occurs underground or inside the enemy's lair. The Hero (and team) face their biggest threat and undergo a metaphorical (and sometimes literal) death and rebirth. Luke and several of his allies are trapped in a trash compactor. Luke is pulled underwater by a creature and almost dies but emerges ready to continue his adventure. Also, Luke witnesses Obi-Wan being struck down, a literal death.

9. **Reward.** The Hero is rewarded for surviving the Ordeal. Luke and his allies escape with the plans for the Death Star and having rescued Princess Leia, who is a rebel.

ACT III

10. **The Road Back.** There's one more big challenge ahead. Luke joins the rebels; they're going to attempt

to take out the Death Star.

11. **Resurrection.** This big challenge includes another metaphorical death and rebirth. After much of the team is taken out, Luke is the last one standing, and the fate of the rebels is in his hands. All seems lost until Han Solo appears and saves the day.

12. **Return with Elixir.** The Hero has successfully completed the journey and can return to the Ordinary World, often bringing an elixir, which can be something that saves the people of the Ordinary World but can also be personal improvement. Luke and Han receive medals for destroying the Death Star.

The Hero's Journey can be used to write stories, troubleshoot stories, or analyze and study stories. It provides us with language for discussing common elements in stories, like the Herald, the Mentor, or the Call to Adventure. Due to its broad appeal and universal nature, the Hero's Journey is one of the most valuable tools for any storyteller to master. For further reading, pick up The Writer's Journey by Christopher Vogler.

Part Four: Practical Considerations

14

Mechanics: Grammar and Formatting

Delving into the rules of grammar is beyond the scope of this book, but it would be remiss to ignore the necessity of mechanically sound writing. Although mechanics aren't specific to storytelling, they are an important part of any form of writing. Many storytellers choose to ignore or downplay the importance of grammar, arguing that readers care more about a compelling story than proper grammar or well-formatted prose. But online bookstores are littered with negative reviews that complain about poorly crafted sentences, bad grammar, inadequate editing, and sloppy formatting. It's true that some readers don't care about the mechanics and may not even notice these flaws in a book, but plenty of readers do care, and they can be vocal about it.

When you follow the rules of grammar in your writing, the work is clear and consistent; therefore, it's easier to read. Messy sentences, grammatical blunders, and haphazard punctuation create roadblocks in your writing that pull readers out of your story. But when a story is written with mechanical competency, the prose flows smoothly and readers can get immersed in the story, resulting in a more enjoyable reading experience and better performance in the marketplace.

Some writers, especially those who dislike editing and have little interest in grammar, argue that it's the responsibility of editors and proofreaders to review the text and fix all the typos and other mistakes. For this reason, some authors don't bother much with learning proper grammar or using it in their prose, which is a detriment to these authors and their works.

When writers submit a manuscript laden with mistakes to an agent or editor, it's tough to get them to read the whole thing, let alone agree to represent or publish the work.

Self-publishing and working with a freelance editor might seem like a viable alternative, but even the best editors in the world cannot catch every mistake in a full-length manuscript, which is why publishers often push books through three, four, or more editors. Most self-published authors can't afford an entire team of editors, so cleaning up the prose becomes even more important for independent authors.

The better the prose is when it lands on the editor's desk, the better they will be able to make it. If a story is rampant with spelling and punctuation errors, the editor may never be able to delve into the content to make deeper edits at the sentence, paragraph, and even chapter levels.

Also, freelance editors might reject a project that reads like a first draft. Most charge by the word, and if the text looks like it's going to take extra time to edit because it's laden with mistakes, they'll either ramp up their rates or reject the job.

There are countless reasons to work on grammar, formatting, and other mechanics of writing. After all, these are the tools of the writer's trade.

Grammar and Orthography

Let's get technical for a minute.

There are two common ways that language manifests: it is either spoken or written. Grammar deals with how we structure sentences and use words, and it is applied to both speech and writing.

Orthography, on the other hand, addresses the rules of a language's writing system or script. Orthography deals with spelling and punctuation, because these elements are only relevant when the language is written. When you say a sentence aloud, you don't say, "period," "question mark," or "exclamation point" at the end of every sentence. However, if you're reading the sentence aloud, you need these punctuation marks to help you navigate the text, and they also provide cues that inform the way we read the text.

Although grammar and orthography are distinct, we usually use *grammar* as an umbrella term that encompasses the rules of language, both spoken and written, and grammar should be understood as inclusive to spelling and punctuation when it's discussed in the context of writing.

Style Guides

Earlier, we talked about literary style as the aesthetics in a written work or across multiple works by one author. But style also refers to any structural considerations that are not addressed by the rules of grammar, spelling, and punctuation.

A serial comma (sometimes called an Oxford comma) is the comma that comes before the conjunction in a list. Here's an example: *I'm going to the bank, the store, and the gas station.* In this sentence, the serial comma is the comma before "and the gas station." We can write the sentence without the serial comma: *I'm going to the bank, the store and the gas station.*

The serial comma is an example of an issue that is not addressed by grammar. *The Associated Press Stylebook (*also called the *AP Stylebook)*, which is widely used in journalism, omits the serial comma unless it's required for comprehension or clarity; traditionally, this was done to save space (and money) in printed magazines and newspapers. However, *The Chicago Manual of Style*, which is the most widely used style guide (especially among fiction editors and publishers), recommends consistent use of the serial comma. Ultimately, use of the serial comma is a stylistic decision left up to the author or editor, and this is just one of many examples of issues that arise in writing, which are not covered by the rules of grammar.

Style guides cover these gaps in the rules of grammar. The aforementioned *Associated Press Stylebook* and *The Chicago Manual of Style* are two such style guides. These style guides offer guidelines that writers can use to ensure that the mechanics of their writing are clear and consistent. Writers who are working toward full-time careers as authors are well served by investing in both grammar resources and style guides.

Formatting

Formatting refers to the design and layout of your manuscript. Which font are you using? Are your chapter headings bold and larger than the body text? Are your lines and paragraphs well spaced? How is the text justified? How wide are the margins? Did you include page numbers?

In early drafts, formatting is not a critical consideration, although keeping your formatting tidy and consistent makes drafting and revising easier on a writer. It's a lot faster to find chapters when the headings are formatted to stand out, and it's more comfortable to look at text that is well spaced on the page.

Formatting becomes more important when you start showing your work around. You might share your outline with a developmental editor. You might show early drafts to alpha readers and later drafts to beta readers. Polished drafts go to an editor. And for the final product, formatting is critical. Readers don't appreciate books and other published works that are sloppy and difficult to navigate.

As with grammar, good formatting makes reading easier and smoother. It allows readers to focus on the story without getting distracted by a sloppy and inconsistent layout.

Mastering Grammar, Orthography, and Formatting

Although many writers find the mechanics of writing tedious, if we spend a little time developing these skills, they soon become second nature. Fortunately, there are some things all writers can do to strengthen their proficiency in these areas.

- **Know what you don't know.** Avoid making assumptions and guesses about grammar. If you're unsure about something, look it up.

- **Spend some time studying grammar.** Pick up a grammar handbook or subscribe to a grammar podcast. You can learn new grammatical rules in a couple of minutes each day.

- **Invest in a style guide.** The Chicago Manual of Style is the recommended style guide for fiction writers. Take a few minutes to look up the answers to your grammar and style questions when they arise.

- **Learn how to use your word processing software so that you can format your documents properly.** You'll find books and tutorials widely available for most applications, especially Scrivener and Microsoft Word, which are the two most widely used applications for authors. It only takes a few hours to learn basic document formatting, and it will save you countless hours and lots of frustration later.

- **Develop good habits by editing e-mails, blog posts, social media updates, and other written communications.** Writers need to practice proofreading and editing, and polished prose strengthens your credibility as a professional writer. Be especially aware of your social media or blog. If your updates are littered with mechanical errors, readers might be discouraged from buying your book.

15

Medium, Format, Tools, and Industry

Medium

Merriam-Webster's dictionary defines *medium* as "a particular form or system of communication...a channel of communication."

Stories abound. They're all around us, and they exist in every medium imaginable. A painting, a photograph, or a sculpture can all tell a story. A song or a dance can tell a story. Stories can be found in ads and speeches, on blogs and social media. Comic books and video games tell stories. And of course, books, plays, movies, and television shows tell stories.

It's impossible to truly master a medium unless you engage with it. As a storyteller, it's critical that you understand your target medium, because each medium has its own rules and limitations. You can do things in a film that you can't do in a novel. Actors will bring characters' facial expressions and body language to life, whereas in novels, body language must be described. Therefore, other means of expression might work better, such as taking readers directly into the characters' thoughts. That's why if you want to make films, you should watch a lot of films, and if you want to write novels, you should read a lot of books.

However, it's also helpful to consume and study stories in

other mediums. If you're a novelist who studies storytelling in books but also in film, you'll soon become acutely aware of the limitations of written the word, because you'll see things on film that you know cannot be executed in a text. Often it is through understanding our limitations that we produce the best work possible.

By absorbing stories in your target medium as well as other mediums, you'll glean a greater understanding of the medium's rules, nuances, and limitations, and you'll be able to better relate to your audience, the people who will eventually consume your stories through that medium. If you don't watch television, how can you create a decent product for people who do? That's like trying to become a musician without ever listening to music.

Most experienced readers can spot a writer who doesn't read. Nonreaders tend to produce choppy text and awkward stories. So get out there and consume stories in every medium you can find, but make sure to pile your plate high with the medium you want to tell stories in.

Format

If you're planning on writing scripts (for film, television, games, or the stage), engaging with the medium won't be enough. You'll also need to read a large number of scripts so that you can see what the story looks like on the page versus the screen or stage. Why? Because medium is a delivery mechanism for stories, but form and format are the tools of design. And for a screenwriter, screenplay is the form and format.

Common forms of prosaic stories include poems, scripts,

novels, and short stories. A script written for the stage uses a different format than a script written for the screen. Screenplays are for movies; teleplays are for television. If you're writing one or the other, then you need to know the difference. Screenplays must follow a very strict format. If an agent or director glances at a script that does not adhere to formatting conventions, then they'll toss it without bothering to read it, because it's an indicator that the screenwriter doesn't know what he or she is doing.

If you're setting out to become a novelist, then you should likewise familiarize yourself with the formatting of a novel. Do you know what front matter and back matter are? What information is included on a copyright page? How many title pages are there? Does the table of contents come before or after the dedication? What's it called when the first letter of a chapter is bigger and more embellished than the other letters?

If you're serious about your craft and truly want to become a professional storyteller, you'll acquire the knowledge necessary to answer these and other questions about your storytelling format.

Tools

It's also helpful to know the tools of your trade, including the ones you don't use. Never underestimate the value of having the right tools at your disposal. Authors once had to write books manually, scrawling every letter onto the page, dipping their pens into inkwells every few words. Making a mistake back then must have been a nightmare!

Having lived through typewriters, word processors, and laptops, I can attest that tools do indeed make a difference. In fact, they can make writing and storytelling faster and simpler because better tools allow you to focus more on story and less on how you're going to fix some silly typo without having to retype an entire chapter.

From note cards for creating a storyboard to mind-mapping and brainstorming apps, from pens and paper to Scrivener and Microsoft Word, familiarizing yourself with the many tools available to you ensures that you will select the tools that will work best for you. This will make your job as a storyteller easier and more enjoyable.

Industry

Are you a play writer or a playwright? Do you have an author bio or an author profile on your website? Do you write prose or verse? Do you know the difference between these and other industry terms?

Each medium, industry, form, and genre has its own jargon, and you won't be able to speak intelligently about your craft unless you learn it. Jargon is a large part of why I wrote this book—to equip fiction writers with the language of storytelling, the terms we use to describe what we do and how we do it.

But learning the jargon isn't enough. You need to know how the industry works. Otherwise, how will your story ever get made?

Selling a screenplay to Hollywood is different from selling a manuscript to a major book publisher. Most agents and publishers expect a full manuscript of a novel to be completed before you submit it; however, if you're writing a nonfiction book, they'll expect a book proposal and a sample chapter. Yet some agents and publishers might deviate from these standards, which is why it's essential that you carefully check their submission guidelines.

If you're writing novels, then you need to understand what's involved in traditional publishing and self-publishing so that you can decide which route is right for you. If you want your book published by a major publishing house, you'll likely need to get an agent first. If you decide to self-publish, you'll need some capital so that you can get your book professionally edited and hire a professional cover designer.

These are the minutia that you need to know. Learning the industry means understanding what steps you need to take and the proper channels you should go through to pitch your story as well as being able to use the proper terminology to discuss these and other industry matters.

Tips for Learning More

Read, watch, and listen to interviews with professionals in your industry, and don't limit yourself to fellow writers. Novelists can learn a lot from film directors and vice versa. Biographies of these professionals can also be useful. Be sure to look for information about agents, editors, publishers, and even cover designers and marketing experts.

Documentaries also provide insight into the industry. I learned a lot about storytelling when I marathon-watched several documentaries about the making of the original *Star Wars* trilogy.

Look for articles online or in print, subscribe to industry publications, and pick up books on both craft and industry. Join a writer's group or attend some local (or online) workshops. Building relationships with other writers is a good way to learn more about the industry.

Most importantly, be curious and know what you don't know. When you hear unfamiliar terms, look them up. I once googled "when the first letter of the chapter is bigger than the other letters." That's how I learned it's called a drop cap.

Once you've obtained knowledge about your industry, stay on top of new developments and trends. Be open in your search for knowledge about your industry and know that learning is a lifelong endeavor.

16

Genre and Audience

Genre is all about the audience. It answers the question of who wants to read this book?

Audiences are looking for a particular type of story based on their moods or personal tastes and interests. We use genre to classify stories and make them easier for audiences to find.

Genre often drives a story's emotional tone. Comedies are funny, dramas are serious, and horrors are scary. Through genre, audiences can determine what type of experience they will get from a story. Some people want lighthearted comedic fare with a touch of romance—they'll find what they're looking for by browsing romantic comedies. Others want a scary experience, a story that has them gripping the edges of their seats—we'll find them in the horror and thriller sections of a bookstore.

Audiences may also be driven by subject matter. They might want a coming-of-age story that is riddled with magic or a high-stakes political mystery. Some want to step back in history and see what it was like to live in the Middle Ages or Ancient Egypt. Others like to stay in the here and now; maybe they're looking for something they can relate to. Genre helps audiences find stories that explore the worlds and subjects that they're interested in.

Genres are also beneficial to authors, making books easier to sell when it's time to market and advertise. The last thing you want to do is market your children's picture book to a young adult audience. Each genre has its own demographic (there's plenty of crossover too). You can post ads for your space opera novel on a *Star Wars* forum or promote your romance story in a place where singles gather.

Genre is also useful for publishers, distributers, bookstores, advertisers, and marketers, as their job is to get stories in front of the target audience. And because authors (especially self-published authors) are responsible for finding their own readers, genre is an incredibly valuable tool.

The Rules of Genre

Each genre has its own set of rules and tropes. For example, a romance must have a happy ending. If a romance doesn't end with the main character walking off into the proverbial sunset, hand in hand with the love of their life, then it's not a romance. Any other ending would make it a love story.

Many writers find genre confining. What if you want to write a funny story about a couple that doesn't end up together? They're going to live happily ever after, but only after they part ways. It's not a romance; it's a love story—but there's no category for love stories! And while it may be a comedy, the comedy genre misses the most important element, which is, in fact, the romance. You can go ahead and call your story a romantic comedy and hope you don't get bombarded with hate mail from readers who are upset that their expectations weren't met, or maybe you'll get lucky and your story will find its audience—maybe you'll even launch a new subgenre. In this sense, genre can limit writers whose ideas fall outside the standard categories we've defined for marketing stories to an audience.

On the other hand, genres can be helpful for storytellers. Working within a set of constraints and writing for a particular audience that has clear expectations can make the process of creating a story easier.

This is why it's important to know your genre. Amateur authors will say they don't read in their genre because they want to be original; they don't want to be influenced by other works. This is a naive approach. An author should enter a genre as an expert. If you don't read in your genre, you run the risk of duplicating great ideas that have already been done. Even storytellers who are well versed in the canon will sometimes repeat ideas without knowing they're doing it.

Suzanne Collins explained that she got the idea for *The Hunger Games* while flipping through TV stations. She saw teenagers competing in a reality show on one channel while teens were killing one another in a war on another channel. The juxtaposition of these images was the impetus for her best-selling trilogy. Her story had similarities to an earlier work called *Battle Royale*, and readers accused her of stealing core concepts from that novel. Even though Collins insists she never read *Battle Royale*, fans still accuse of her stealing from it. For the record, I believe Ms. Collins. Although none of the fuss surrounding the similarities between *Battle Royale* and *The Hunger Games* hurt her career, it's an accusation than can often be avoided by simply familiarizing yourself with the canon in which you want to work. If you write science fiction but have never immersed yourself in the genre, you'll look pretty silly when you think you've come up with the original idea of laser swords, which fans will immediately recognize as the lightsabers of *Star Wars*.

Although you could never read every work in your genre, and you always run the risk of putting something distinct in your story that has been done before, it's important to be familiar with the major works and storytellers in your field.

Consumers of genre have strict expectations from storytellers, but genre is not always clear cut. Fans are still arguing about whether 1977's *Star Wars: A New Hope* is fantasy or science fiction. Some say it's fantasy because they see magic in the story. Others say the science-fiction elements (spaceships, interplanetary travel, and a galactic empire) outweigh the magic and make it a sci-fi flick. *Star Wars* is a fairy tale in space, which classifies it as fantasy, but it's also a space opera, which is a subgenre of science fiction. It's one of those stories that defies the boundaries of genre, and it does so quite successfully.

Genres are constantly changing, merging, evolving, and emerging. Two different bookstores will present two different sets of genres, but it's a good idea to know the basics: literary fiction; romance; mystery, thriller, and suspense; science fiction; fantasy; horror; children's and young adult; and historical are the major genres in literature.

And then there are subgenres, which are niche categories within each genre. As an example, romance has many subgenres: clean and wholesome, contemporary, erotica, inspirational, historical, and romantic comedy, to name a few. It's not enough to study romance broadly—if you're writing historical romance, you need to dig into that subgenre. Get to know the books and authors in that category. Study the stories so that you understand what readers want, what's already been done, and what opportunities are available for a fresh take in the subgenre.

Literary Fiction and Everything Else

Every industry has its snobs, and storytelling is certainly no exception. You'll find snobs in every genre: sci-fi fans will roll their eyes if you've never read Dune. Romance fans will drop their jaws if you haven't read a Nora Roberts book. And horror fans will gasp if you say Stephen King isn't for you.

But there's no greater divide than the one that exists between literary fiction and everything else. So what does that mean? Isn't all fiction considered literary? Yes and no.

In fact, literary fiction (lit fic for short) is so at odds with all other genres that some writers simply say they are either literary fiction writers or genre writers. Being a genre writer means you write something other than literary fiction.

Because literary fiction is set apart from every other genre, and because this is where you'll find most works in a culture's literary tradition and canon, it's important to understand what it is and why it's important—and why some people think it's superior to genre storytelling.

Literary fiction encompasses works that are considered to hold literary merit, which indicates critical acclaim. These works tend to be of a serious nature and often explore the complexities of the human condition in meaningful ways. Literary fiction can also be experimental or artistic, and it's diligent in its craftsmanship with regard to language and structure.

But wait a minute—can't romance or science fiction hold literary merit? Can't genre fiction be complex and meaningful? Can't it explore the human condition? Yes, of course! That's why some genre stories cross over into the lit-fic category. Ray Bradbury's Fahrenheit 451 is an example of a sci-fi book that did just that, and that was after years of Bradbury suffering torment from literary peers who looked down on his work as pulp. People didn't take him seriously, but in the end, he showed them.

Genre for Storytellers

So how do you become familiar with all the genres? Easy: you consume, study, and practice. But your focus should certainly be within the genre you want to write.

Look for books, movies, and television shows in your genre, and get to know them all—the classics, the contemporary hits, and the cult favorites. Study your genre too. If you can find books or documentaries about your genre, read and watch them. As you explore your genre, pay attention to the commonalities. What are the defining features of your genre? Can a storyteller get away with bending or breaking genre rules? What happens when you throw some fantasy into your sci-fi story? What if your horror story is hilarious?

Be sure to get to know the masters in your genre as well, the Stephen Kings, Ray Bradburys, and Nora Robertses.

Become an expert in your genre, but don't ignore the other genres! All genres inform each other, and when authors get too absorbed in a single type of story, the work often lacks balance. The sci-fi writer becomes too focused on tech and gadgets. The romance author is more interested in love scenes than in the characters' development.

Some storytellers simply cannot abide by writing to

genre, and that's fine. If you're inspired or have an artistic vision that you want to explore, then your best course of action will be to pursue that vision. However, you should still familiarize yourself with the genres to gain a basic understanding of what each entails.

Part Five: Story Scholarship

17

Studying Stories

One of the best ways to learn the art of storytelling is through careful study of the stories you read. By examining their structure and content, you can deepen your knowledge and understanding of the craft, and you will develop a more intuitive approach to storytelling over time.

At first, reading stories from a writer's perspective might feel clinical as you try to break every story into its various components. This can make it harder to enjoy stories as sheer entertainment. Instead of relaxing and taking it in, you'll be looking for plot points and character arcs, trying to identify the stages of the Hero's Journey. Some people find this a more enjoyable way to consume stories; others miss being entertained. Every once in a while, you can turn off your analytical mind and enjoy the ride.

This practice of story scholarship will also raise your standards. A natural side effect of story analysis will make you a critical reader. It will become harder to find stories that blow your mind, because now you've seen what happens behind the scenes. Now you know what differentiates a great story from a mediocre story.

In the end, you'll find that excellence in storytelling is quite rare, and you'll learn to appreciate the strong elements of a story while viewing the weaker elements with a critical eye. And eventually you'll be able to study and enjoy stories simultaneously and holistically.

Story Study Tips

As you read stories, do so from the perspective of a storyteller. Consider the options that were at the storyteller's disposal. For example, if a character is betrayed by a loved one, there are several choices available to that character: confront the loved one, seek revenge, or cut off ties. Ask yourself why the storyteller made specific choices for the direction of the story. What storytelling opportunities are gained by a character who seeks revenge as opposed to a character who cuts off ties with someone who betrayed them? Would you have done things differently? Would a different choice lead to the same outcome?

Pay close attention to characters in stories. Why do some characters make you feel like you've known them all your life? What is it about some characters that you don't like, even though they haven't done anything wrong? What makes some characters forgettable and other characters memorable? Could any characters have been left out of the story without changing its core? Would adding characters to a story strengthen it?

Look for characters who embody various archetypes from the Hero's Journey. The Hero will be obvious, but can you find the Herald? The Mentor? A Shapeshifter? Do any of the characters embody two or more archetypes? Do characters carry out the archetypal functions, or did the storyteller use alternative methods, such as using a book of wisdom as the Mentor?

Take note of important story moments. What image was depicted in the opening scene? How does it compare to the image at the story's closing? What occurred at the midpoint?

How does the narrative build up to high-tension moments? How is the story paced? Where do the emotional turns occur, and how does their placement contribute to the story's tone and flow?

Watch for plot points. Although plot points aren't universal, there are a few that appear in the vast majority of stories. For example, make it a habit to watch for the inciting incident and the breaks into acts two and three.

Make predictions about where a story is going, and see if you're correct. Also, note how you feel when you guess correctly. Is the story predictable in a disappointing way or in a satisfying way? Did the story surprise you? Were the surprises believable, or did you feel they were placed in the story for shock value?

Believability is an important aspect of storytelling, even in stories that are populated with aliens and mythological creatures. A skilled writer makes readers believe the impossible, even if only for the duration of the story. This is especially essential for science fiction, fantasy, and horror. When reading these kinds of books, do you find yourself rolling your eyes and thinking, *Yeah, right, that would never happen,* or are you caught up in the action? How did the narrative pull you into its fantastical world? Did it use rich and believable characters? Was the story world vivid, detailed, and easy to visualize?

Studying successful stories will show you what works, but it can be just as useful to consider the flaws in stories that don't work. Examine parts of stories that are weak. This will show you what to avoid in your own work. Was it something about the characters? Was the plot half-baked? Were there issues with continuity or believability? Was the pacing off?

Was the tone inconsistent? Did you find any plot holes?

Learn to articulate the strengths and weaknesses in the stories you consume, and you will vastly improve your own storytelling skills. An excellent way to study stories is to conduct a story analysis.

Story Analysis

In the following sections, you'll find a story analysis followed by a structural breakdown that identifies the three acts as well as the archetypes and stages of the Hero's Journey. For the story analysis, we'll look at L. Frank Baum's novel, *The Wonderful Wizard of Oz*. However, for the structural breakdown, we'll look at the 1939 film adaptation, *The Wizard of Oz*.

It's useful to look at both the book and the movie to see how film adaptations deviate from source material. Sometimes changes are made by directors who want to alter the story and make it their own. Other times, the medium of film won't accommodate certain elements of a written narrative, because there are things that can be done in writing that won't work in film and vice versa. Studying both versions allows us to examine some of the differences between these two mediums, and we can learn a thing or two about what's involved in adapting a book to a movie, which is especially useful for authors who hope to see their own works turned into films someday.

Watching movies is usually a faster and easier way to consume and study stories than reading novels. You can watch a movie in a fraction of the time it takes to read a book, so the storytelling is tight and concise. However, reading and studying written stories is critical for authors who want to tell stories with the written word. I recommend reading the book and watching the film to get the most out of the analyses that follow.

Analyses tend to vary, depending on who's doing the analyzing. If you conduct your own analysis, you might find a different theme in the novel. You might disagree with whether a character is secondary or tertiary. You might identify a different Herald or Mentor. Maybe you view a character as a Shadow that another analysis views as an Ally. One of the great things about art and storytelling is that we each get to make our own interpretations. Have fun with it!

18

Story Analysis: *The Wonderful Wizard of Oz* (Novel)

Now that we've gathered the building blocks of storytelling, let's examine a story and see if we can identify its parts. To make our story analysis a little easier, we'll be using a worksheet. You can find a blank template of this worksheet in appendix A, and you can use it to conduct your own story analyses of books and movies as you continue your storytelling studies independently.

We'll use L. Frank Baum's classic children's novel *The Wonderful Wizard of Oz* to conduct our story analysis. This book is in the public domain, and you should be able to pick up a copy at any bookstore or library, or for free on any e-reader or mobile device. In the next chapter, we'll use the film adaptation of this book to conduct a structural analysis of the story.

Title: *The Wonderful Wizard of Oz*

Author: L. Frank Baum

Medium: Book/novel

Genre: Children's fantasy

Concept: A girl is swept away to a fantastical wonderland called Oz.

Premise: An orphan being raised on her aunt and uncle's

farm is carried away by a cyclone to a fantastical land, where she sets out on an adventure to find her way home. Along the way, she finds herself.

Characters

Protagonist: Dorothy

Antagonist: There are multiple antagonists, including the infamous Wicked Witch of the West. Various other creatures serve as antagonists, many of whom don't appear in the film (such as the Hammer-Heads), and often nature or the environment functions as an antagonist.

Other primary characters: Scarecrow, Tin Woodsman, Cowardly Lion

Secondary characters: Toto, Uncle Henry, Aunt Em, Wizard of Oz, Good Witch of the North, Glinda

Tertiary characters: Munchkins

Note: There are dozens of characters in *The Wonderful Wizard of Oz*; many function somewhere between tertiary and secondary characters.

Describe the protagonist's internal struggle and external goal. Dorothy's external goal is to get home. Her internal struggle is learning to believe in herself and to act with intelligence, kindness, and courage; these are the traits she needs in order to find her way home.

Describe the protagonist's character arc. Dorothy learns that she has what it takes to get home. She does this by incorporating the traits of her allies (intelligence, kindness, and courage).

Describe one to three key relationships and how they develop.

- Aunt Em and Uncle Henry. Dorothy learns to appreciate her home and her family.

- Scarecrow, Tin Woodsman, and Cowardly Lion. Dorothy develops close bonds and strong friendships with these characters. These relationships help Dorothy develop intelligence, kindness, and courage.

- Wizard of Oz. Dorothy is submissive to Oz when she meets him, but when she learns he's a phony, he becomes the inferior one in the relationship. By the end, there is mutual respect and forgiveness on Dorothy's part.

Plot

Summarize the plot (core conflict) in fewer than five hundred words.

Dorothy lives in a dull, gray world surrounded by poverty and bland, ordinary people. When a cyclone hits, Dorothy is busy chasing her dog Toto and doesn't make it to the storm cellar in time. The cyclone carries the house, with Dorothy and Toto inside, to a lush, vibrant, and colorful land called Oz.

Dorothy is greeted by the Good Witch of the North and learns that her house has landed on a wicked witch; she has inadvertently killed the witch, liberating a people called Munchkins, who were under the witch's dominion. She is rewarded with beautiful silver shoes. But Dorothy wants to go home, so she sets off on a yellow brick road, which will take her to the Wizard of Oz; he may be the only one in the land who can help her get home.

During her journey, Dorothy meets three important new friends: the Scarecrow, the Tin Woodsman, and the Cowardly Lion. All three join her because they too want something from the wizard: brains, a heart, and courage (respectively).

Throughout their adventures, they encounter many dangers and overcome a variety of adversaries. Eventually they reach Oz, and the wizard promises to fulfill their requests if they kill the Wicked Witch of the West. They do so and return to Oz, but the wizard delays fulfilling his end of the bargain. Angry, they demand their requests be fulfilled. Then they learn he's not a wizard at all, just a man who's fooling everyone.

The wizard regrets his deception and does his best to grant their wishes. However, getting Dorothy home proves to be a challenge. He attempts to bring her home in a hot air balloon, but as she's boarding, her dog Toto runs off. Dorothy chases Toto, and the balloon takes off without her.

Dorothy is crushed that she cannot go home, but then a good witch appears and tells Dorothy the silver slippers are magical and will take her home. She had what she needed to get home the whole time!

After heartfelt goodbyes to her new friends, Dorothy returns to Kansas as a wiser person who has incorporated the traits of thoughtfulness (or intelligence), kindness, and courage. She is now self-actualized.

Identify one to three subplots.

- The other primary characters (Scarecrow, Tin Woodsman, and Cowardly Lion) are on their own quests to have their wishes fulfilled by the Wizard of Oz.

- The Wicked Witch of the West wants to get the silver shoes from Dorothy.

List five to ten narrative techniques used in the story.

- Allegory. The Scarecrow is a symbol of Dorothy's intelligence; the Tin Woodsman is a symbol of Dorothy's kindness; and the Cowardly Lion is a symbol of her courage. The entire story is an allegory for Dorothy developing these traits within herself.

- Dramatic visualization. There are many lengthy descriptions throughout the story.

- Oxymoron. The name of one of the primary characters is an oxymoron: the Cowardly Lion.

- Pathos. Dorothy uses emotional appeal to convince other characters to help her get home.

- Symbol. The shoes Dorothy receives are a symbol of the journey she takes on foot.

Setting

Describe the story's setting.

The story starts at a farm on the drab, gray Kansas prairie. Dorothy later finds herself in the lush, colorful, and magical land of Oz.

Theme

What is the main theme of the story? Be kind, smart, and brave.

Try to identify at least three other themes in the story.

- Friendship and loyalty to others build character

- Appreciation of home and family

- Belief in oneself

Style and Voice

What is the tense and point of view? Third-person past tense. The narrative varies from subjective to objective (sometimes calling the characters "our friends"). The point of view is mostly limited as the story almost always stays with Dorothy, but there are a few scenes that depart from her, such as when the Scarecrow, Tin Woodsman, and Cowardly Lion visit the wizard, each alone and without Dorothy.

How would you describe the narrative voice? Clear, simple, descriptive, and age appropriate for a children's book.

Critical Analysis

Considering the basic building blocks of effective storytelling, how does this story measure up? Describe three strengths and three weaknesses in the storytelling.

Strengths

- The characters are realistic and interesting, even though many are fantastical.

- The story stays focused on the central plot: Dorothy's desire to get home (and finding herself along the way).

- The world building is magnificent and imaginative. Where most fantasies use familiar worlds based on the Middle Ages, Baum came up with a fresh and exciting story world.

Weaknesses

- Lack of balance. The Scarecrow and Tin Woodsman have elaborate backstories, but the Cowardly Lion does not.

- Too many characters. This is especially noticeable when the novel is compared to the film adaptation, which has fewer characters who function better. For example, the film worked better with one good witch instead of two.

- Too many pit stops. Although the movie could have used more material from the book, the book could have been more concise with fewer plot points along the journey, especially the porcelain land, which didn't add anything essential to the story.

19

Story Structure Analysis: *The Wizard of Oz* (Film)

In examining and studying story structure, we'll stay with L. Frank Baum's classic, but we'll use the 1939 film adaptation *The Wizard of Oz*. We'll plug *The Wizard of Oz* into both the three-act structure and the Hero's Journey.

The Three-Act Structure in The Wizard of Oz (Film)

Act I: Setup

We meet an orphaned farm girl named Dorothy who lives with her aunt and uncle on the drab, gray Kansas prairie. She wants to go "somewhere over the rainbow," someplace better. The first conflict occurs when a grumpy neighbor named Miss Gulch takes away Dorothy's dog Toto. Toto escapes and returns to Dorothy, who decides to run away to save her dog. While on the road, Dorothy encounters Professor Marvel, who convinces her to return home just as a tornado is brewing. This leads to the second conflict (and inciting incident): Dorothy doesn't make it to the storm cellar in time, so she runs into the house and is swept away by the tornado. The first act ends by raising the dramatic question of whether Dorothy will ever return home.

Act II: Conflict

Dorothy lands in a faraway and fantastical land called Oz, which is lush, vibrant, and colorful. However, Dorothy sticks with her decision to return home. A good witch called Glinda gives her a pair of ruby slippers and tells Dorothy to go see the Wizard of Oz, in the Emerald City, who may be able to help her get home.

Throughout the second act, Dorothy acquires friends and helpers and faces her antagonist, the Wicked Witch of the West, who wants to "get" Dorothy and take her shoes (we don't know it yet, but these are the magic shoes she'll need to get home, so the witch is after the one thing Dorothy needs to fulfill her goal).

Dorothy's friends represent traits that she needs to develop. These include intellect or thoughtfulness (brains), kindness (heart), and courage. She uses these skills to get out of various situations and solve problems that she faces.

Dorothy and her friends make it to the Emerald City, where the great and powerful Oz promises to fulfill their wishes if they kill the Wicked Witch of the West and bring her broom to him.

Act III: Resolution

The climax occurs when Dorothy kills the Wicked Witch, eliminating the threat to the shoes, which will later prove to be Dorothy's only way home. Dorothy then returns to Oz. The wizard turns out to be a fraud. He attempts to take her home to Kansas, but she fails to make it to the hot air balloon before it takes off, because Toto has run off and she's chasing him. All seems lost, but then Glinda the Good Witch appears and explains that Dorothy can use the shoes to get home. Dorothy clicks her heels together three times, says, "There's no place like home," and returns to Kansas.

The Hero's Journey in The Wizard of Oz (Film)

Archetypes

Hero: Dorothy
Herald: Toto
Mentor: Professor Marvel, Glinda the Good Witch of the North
Threshold Guardian(s): The door of Dorothy's house (she crosses through it to enter Oz); the guard at the gates of the Emerald City
Shadow: Miss Gulch, Wicked Witch of the West
Shapeshifter: The Wizard of Oz
Trickster: Munchkins (comic relief)
Allies: Scarecrow, Tin Man, Cowardly Lion

Act I: Departure

1. *Ordinary World.* Dorothy lives on a farm in the drab, gray Kansas prairie. She yearns to go someplace better, somewhere "over the rainbow."
2. *Call to Adventure.* The grumpy neighbor, Miss Gulch, takes away Dorothy's dog Toto because he's been digging up her flowers. Toto escapes from Miss Gulch and flees back to Dorothy, who decides they'll have to run away or Toto will never be safe.
3. *Meeting with the Mentor.* While on the road, Dorothy encounters Professor Marvel, who convinces Dorothy

that she's needed at home.

4. *Refusal of the Call*. Dorothy decides to return home.

5. *Crossing the Threshold to the Special World*. A tornado is brewing. By the time Dorothy gets back to the farm, the family and farmhands are already in the storm cellar. Dorothy enters the house right before it's swept up in the tornado, eventually landing in a colorful world called Oz. There, Dorothy meets the Munchkins and Glinda, the Good Witch of the North. Glinda gives Dorothy a talisman (the ruby slippers) and advice to go see the Wizard of Oz, because he's the only one who might be able to return Dorothy to Kansas. Wearing the slippers, Dorothy embarks on her journey down the Yellow Brick Road.

Act II: Initiation

6. *Tests, Allies, and Enemies*. Dorothy acquires three allies, each of whom wants something from the Wizard of Oz: the Scarecrow desires brains, the Tinman seeks a heart, and the Cowardly Lion desires courage. The Wicked Witch of the West becomes Dorothy's enemy. As Dorothy and her new friends journey to Oz, they face many tests: attacks from the witch, poison flowers, and evil trees. When they finally get to the Emerald City, the great and powerful Oz says he'll grant their wishes if they kill the Wicked Witch of the West; to prove they've completed this task, they must bring him the witch's broom.

7. *Approach to the Inmost Cave*. The travelers approach the castle of the Wicked Witch of the West.

8. *Ordeal*. Dorothy's friends are overtaken and she is

brought into the witch's castle as a prisoner. Using an hourglass, the witch curses Dorothy to death.

9. *Reward.* Dorothy's friends show up and rescue her. They kill the witch and get the broom.

Act III: Return

10. *The Road Back.* Dorothy and her Allies bring the broom to the Wizard of Oz, but he cannot grant Dorothy's wish. The great wizard turns out to be a fraud.

11. *Resurrection.* In an attempt to redeem himself, the wizard plans to take Dorothy home in a hot-air balloon. However, the balloon takes off without Dorothy. It seems Dorothy has missed her only chance to return to Kansas, but then Glinda appears and tells Dorothy how to get home using the ruby slippers.

12. *Return with Elixir.* Dorothy returns home with a new appreciation for her family and a more developed sense of self.

Part Six: Using These Building Blocks

20

Putting It All Together: Best Practices for Storytellers

Many experienced authors (as well as agents, editors, and scholars) have developed and shared their storytelling processes, methodologies, and systems, which have been widely adopted by novice writers. Some of these systems are designed to boost your creativity, while others provide methods for developing plots, characters, settings, themes, and other story elements. Some show you how to fix problems in your stories; others show you how to structure stories.

Occasionally, you'll encounter writing gurus who will tell you exactly how to write a story. They'll outline every step of the process and provide you with guides and worksheets, sometimes drilling down into scene-by-scene formulas. Some will even claim that theirs is the only correct way to write a story, or they'll promise that if you use their method, your story will succeed.

However, there is no right or wrong way to write a story. The wide variety of popular stories and the broad range of storytelling processes is a testament to that fact. Writers are free to turn their ideas into stories any way they want. There are writers who outline and writers who work without a plan. Some authors jump around in a story's timeline as they produce a draft. Others write stories from beginning to end.

Some edit as they go. Others produce a rough draft, then a series of revisions until they reach the final polish. Some writers use established structures and formulas; others write intuitively. As you study the craft of storytelling, experiment with various techniques and systems, and you will eventually develop a process that works best for you. But always remember that what works for one author—or even thousands of authors—will not be ideal for everyone.

You'll find your tools and develop your own process by studying the craft of storytelling. You can read books on craft, subscribe to blogs, listen to podcasts, and look for interviews with authors. And of course, consume plenty of stories. All of these resources will fill up your writer's toolbox.

Best Practices for Storytellers

On more than one occasion, writing gurus have advised novices that writing stories should be fun. "If you're not having fun, you're doing something wrong." This is, in my opinion, half-baked advice. Yes, storytelling should be fun, but there will be moments when you don't feel like doing the work. At times you'll get stuck, frustrated, or grow tired of your project. That's why we use the terms *art* and *work* interchangeably. Many failed storytellers can't get past the stages of creativity that are fun and exciting. When it's time to hunker down and push through the difficult parts, they lose interest. Completing a novel is a remarkable accomplishment, especially if it's a good story (and you'll probably write a lot of mediocre stories before producing a good one). Any accomplishment worth achieving requires putting in the time and energy. Some stages of the journey are fun, but others will be a struggle, so prepare yourself for the hard work and discipline that will be required in order to succeed.

Fortunately, many people have succeeded before us, and we can learn from their successes, failures, and experiences. We can pull together some of the practices that have been proven to lead to success.

- **Write every day.** Most full-time working writers find that their best work and productivity happens when they write on a daily schedule. It's like exercising: to stay in shape, you've got to work out regularly.

- **Consume stories, and read within your genre.** When you're a writer who doesn't read, it shows in your work. Reading helps you absorb language and story, and it shows you what works and what doesn't work, saving you a lot of time in revisions. You can also learn about storytelling from reading stories as well as watching films and television with a critical eye.

- **Practice makes perfect**. Don't be too hard on yourself. The first few stories you write probably won't be publishable. The first few stories you publish probably won't sell millions of copies or win a Pulitzer Prize. Like any craft, it takes time to master storytelling. Give yourself space to learn, study, experiment, and practice.

- **Finish what you start.** One of the most common blights on writers is the shiny new idea. You're working on a story, but it's been a few months, and it's starting to get old. Then one day you get another shiny new idea, and you abandon your original project. For most writers, this leads to a stack of unfinished projects and a permanent job in a cubicle. Push through those times when a project loses its luster, and trust that your passion for it will eventually resume. Some writers find that working on two projects simultaneously helps keep their interest and momentum moving. You can also focus on one primary project and set aside time each day for whatever inspires you.

- **There are exceptions when projects should be cast away.** Many first novels are treated as practice runs, and it's not a bad idea to write your first novel with zero intent on publishing. This removes a lot of pressure. Other projects may not pan out. If you've spent countless months on a novel but the story isn't working, then maybe the problems run too deep to be fixed. The trick is to avoid chasing shiny new ideas and dropping projects out of boredom—especially during the revision process, which many writers find tedious. Try to drop projects only when you're certain you can't bring them to reasonable completion.

- **Study the craft.** Read books on writing. Save articles on storytelling. Watch interviews and listen to podcasts featuring experienced and successful storytellers. Never before in history have we had access to so much knowledge. Use it to your advantage!

- **Learn the industry and be professional.** Those who are lucky and hardworking enough to become full-time authors are running businesses, and they treat their work like the business it is. Successful businesses cannot be run on artistry alone. We can be artists when we write and businesspeople when we're running reports, tracking sales, and setting up marketing campaigns. Writing is only half the battle. Understanding the publishing industry and marketplace will improve our chances for success.

- **Learn the differences between self-publishing and traditional publishing.** There is much debate about whether it's better to self-publish or find a traditional publisher. By understanding what's involved in both and learning about the benefits and drawbacks of each, you can make an informed decision about which route is best for you.

Storytelling is an enlightening and rewarding experience whether you're doing it for fun or to build a career. As you progress through your journey, I hope you'll find the concepts and tools provided in this book useful, and I hope you'll continue to stock your writer's toolbox with methods, processes, and techniques that will help you become the best storyteller possible. Good luck, and keep writing those stories!

Appendix A: Worksheets

Story Analysis Worksheet

Title:
Author (or Director):
Medium:
Genre:

Concept:
Premise:

Logline:

Characters

Protagonist:
Antagonist:
Other primary characters:
Secondary characters:
Tertiary characters:

Describe the protagonist's external goal and internal struggle.

Describe the protagonist's character arc.

Describe one to three key relationships and how they develop.

Plot

Summarize the plot (core conflict) in fewer than five hundred words.

Identify one to three subplots.

List five to ten narrative techniques used in the story.

Can you identify a structure (three-act structure, Hero's Journey, etc.)? If so, write a brief overview explaining how the story adhered to the structure.

Setting

Describe the story's setting.

Theme

What is the main theme of the story?

Try to identify at least three other themes in the story.

Style and Voice

What is the tense and point of view?

How would you describe the narrative voice?

Critical Analysis

Considering the basic building blocks of effective storytelling, how does this story measure up? Describe three strengths and three weaknesses in the storytelling.

Character Sketch Worksheet

This template is designed to encourage you to think about characters in depth. You can use it to analyze a character from a book or film, or you can use it to create a character for a story of your own.

Character Arc

What does the character want (external goal)?

Why does the character want this?

What is preventing the character from getting what they want?

What are the stakes?

What is the character's internal struggle, and how is it preventing them from getting what they want?

How does the character need to change and grow to get what he or she wants?

Personality

What does the character love?

What does the character fear?

What are the character's strengths?

What are the character's weaknesses?

Describe the character's behavior and attitude.

Describe the character's style and tastes, likes and dislikes.

Physical Description

List the character's age, height, weight, and hair and eye color.

List the character's facial and physical features.

What is the character's ethnicity or heritage?

Background

Education:

Skills:

Occupation:

Interests:

Beliefs (politics/religion):

Significant life events:

Miscellaneous

Does the character fill an archetypal role in the story?

Describe the character's key relationships (friends, family, coworkers, enemies).

Write a few paragraphs of the character's backstory.

Describe the beginning, middle, and end of this character's arc.

Write a few paragraphs in the character's voice.

Story Structure Worksheets

The following two worksheets are for analyzing or developing stories.

The Three-Act Structure

Act I: Setup

Introduce the characters, their relationships, and the story world.

What is the protagonist's goal and what's holding them back?

The protagonist is faced with a conflict.

Dealing with this conflict leads to a second and more significant conflict (inciting incident), which presents a dramatic and permanent change for the protagonist, raising the central story question or challenge.

Act II: Conflict

How do the stakes get higher? How does the tension increase?

The protagonist attempts to tackle the challenge or solve the problem at the heart of the story. These attempts cause the situation to worsen.

Along the way there are successes and failures.

The protagonist does not possess the skills or traits necessary and must acquire them.

What is the climax, the most intense moment of the story, when conflict, tension, and stakes are at their highest?

Act III: Resolution

How does the central story problem (main plot) and all subplots get resolved?

How has the protagonist (and possibly the other characters as well as the story world) changed from who and where they were in the beginning?

The Hero's Journey

Archetypes

1. Hero:
2. Herald:
3. Mentor:
4. Threshold Guardian:
5. Shadow:
6. Shapeshifter:
7. Trickster:
8. Allies:

Act I: Departure

1. Ordinary World:
2. Call to Adventure:
3. Refusal of the Call:
4. Meeting with the Mentor:
5. Crossing the First Threshold:

Act II: Initiation

6. Tests, Allies, and Enemies:
7. Approach to the Inmost Cave:
8. Ordeal:
9. Reward:

Act III: Return

10. The Road Back:
11. Resurrection:
12. Return with Elixir:

Glossary of Literary Devices and Narrative Techniques

This list of literary devices and narrative techniques is not exhaustive. There are many literary devices that deal with specific types of writing, such as poetry or rhetoric, but are not especially valuable in storytelling. Further study of literary devices and narrative techniques will strengthen your mastery of language.

Allegory. A narrative with a hidden meaning, which often imparts a moral lesson. "The Tortoise and the Hare" is an allegory about a tortoise who beats a hare in a race, demonstrating that natural talent or skill without effort is no match for persistence, focus, and hard work.

Alliteration. Two consonant sounds used in close proximity, especially the first letters of two consecutive words. The phrase *cookie cutter* uses alliteration with the hard C at the beginning of each word. Alliteration can also exist within a single word, such as the B sound in *blueberry*.

Amplification. When language is embellished to assert or increase the importance of a topic. For example: it's a gorgeous day; the sun is shining bright, there isn't a cloud in the beautiful blue sky, and the birds are singing in joyous harmony.

Anagram. The letters of a word, phrase, or sentence are rearranged to form a new word, phrase, or sentence. The word *begin* is an anagram of *being*.

Anthropomorphism. When a nonhuman character (including plants and animals as well as inanimate objects) is given sentience or humanlike traits and abilities, such as talking.

Assonance. A vowel sound is repeated in close proximity. For example, the O sound is repeated in the word *rollover*.

Asyndeton. Omission of conjunctions. For example, in the phrase *I came, I saw, I left,* there are no conjunctions.

Author surrogate. A fictional character who is based on the author.

Backstory. Events that occurred prior to the current story. Authors often create backstories for their characters to gain a deeper understanding of them; events from backstories may or may not be revealed in the main story.

Bathos. A sudden change in style or voice, usually from elegant or lofty to vulgar or ridiculous. Bathos can occur unintentionally, or it can be used intentionally, usually for humor.

Breaking the fourth wall. The narrator breaks character to speak directly to the audience. It's often used for humor or to make the audience feel like they're in on the jokes.

Character arc. The growth and development that a character undergoes throughout the course of a story.

Character voice. The distinct way a character speaks in dialogue as differentiated from the other characters.

Chekhov's gun. A principle in storytelling that says if you show a gun in the first act of a play, it must be fired in the next act. If something in a scene seems important, then it needs to be used in the story to fulfill reader expectations.

Cliffhanger. A scene, chapter, book, or other installment that ends at a critical moment, such as when a character is hanging off the edge of a cliff.

Comic relief. A moment of humor that occurs in a story that would not be classified in the humor or comedy genres. Comic relief is used to ease tension and break up lengthy sequences of intense drama, tragedy, suspense, or horror.

Connotation. The nonliteral meaning or emotional subtext of a word. *Childish* and *childlike* are synonyms, but *childish* has a negative connotation and is often used as an insulting way to describe immature behavior, whereas *childlike* is often used to describe behavior that is innocent or full of awe and wonder.

Deathtrap. A plot device in which the antagonist has captured the protagonist (or other primary sympathetic characters) to murder them, and there appears to be no way out.

Defamiliarization. Familiar people, objects, or events are presented in an unfamiliar way. The original example is from Tolstoy's *Kholstomer,* featuring a horse as narrator, which defamiliarized readers with the story world.

Denotation. The literal meaning of a word (as opposed to a word's implied meaning or secondary definitions).

Denouement. The final scenes of a story, after the climax, in which the plot and all subplots are resolved and all story questions are answered.

Deus ex machina. A difficult or impossible situation in a story is resolved through unlikely or unbelievable methods, often through supernatural intervention.

Distancing effect. Intentionally crafting a character so that the audience doesn't oversympathize, often used so that the audience will approach the character with scrutiny or cynicism.

Dramatic visualization. An abundance of descriptive, visual detail or use of extensive action (such as gestures and facial expressions with dialogue) to make the narrative more visual and easier for readers to imagine.

Dream sequence. The narrative depicts a character's dream played out as a scene or series of scenes.

Echo. In language, a repetition of a sound or syllable; in storytelling, the repetition of a motif, theme, or event.

Epistolary. A story that is written as a series of letters or other documents, such as memos.

Ethos. A persuasive appeal using ethics or morality, often used to establish a speaker's credibility.

Eucatastrophe. The protagonist is facing a pending catastrophic event, which is overcome and turns out to be beneficial for the protagonist.

Euphuism. Language that is artificially elegant and often overstuffed with literary devices.

Flashback. The narrative jumps back in time and shows a scene from the past.

Flash-forward. The narrative jumps forward in time and shows a scene from the future.

Flashing arrow. In film, an audiovisual cue draws the audience's attention to something that seems benign but will be important later.

Foreshadowing. A scene, event, or character reflects (or hints at) what will happen later in the story.

Frame story. A story that contains one or more stories within it. The film *Titanic* uses a frame story, with Old Rose recounting what happened to her younger self aboard the ill-fated ship.

Framing device. Actions, scenes, and events that bookend a story and are used to establish it as a frame for inner stories.

Hamartia. Often associated with Greek tragedies, a character's flaw or mistake results in a reversal of fortune. Essentially, it's the consequences of characters making bad decisions.

Head jumping. The narrative is inside a character's thoughts and then jumps to another character's thoughts, often in a manner that is unclear and leaves the reader confused.

Hyperbole. Using exaggeration to evoke strong feelings, agreement, or sympathy.

Imagery. Text that evokes images in the reader's mind.

Inciting incident. The incident or event that kicks off the story's core conflict, challenge, or problem, usually occurring after the protagonist or primary characters have been introduced.

Info dump. Short for *information dump*; a lengthy passage revealing information that is relevant to the story, such as when the narrative explains the history of the story world to impart necessary background information to the reader.

In media res. The narrative begins in the middle of the story's action. In media res is often used for nonlinear storytelling.

Irony. Events or situations are contrary to what one would expect.

Leitwortstil. Repetition of words or phrases to emphasize a symbol, theme, or motif in a story.

Linear storytelling. The story follows a chronological order of events.

Logos. A persuasive appeal using logic and reason.

Love triangle. Three characters have romantic feelings for one another in any combination.

MacGuffin. The protagonist is pursuing a goal or is on a quest for unknown reasons. The MacGuffin is common in quests, mysteries, and thrillers. The object of the hero's goal or quest is the MacGuffin.

Magical realism. Magic exists in a real-world setting (as opposed to a fantastical world).

Mary Sue. A type of author surrogate who is an idealized version of the author. Mary Sue is also used to describe characters who are flawless, overly skilled, and without weaknesses.

Metaphor. Presenting one thing as something else, usually for demonstrative purposes: *she is a rock*.

Metonymy. Using a word to mean something that the word refers to rather than what it actually means. In the quote, "The pen is mightier than the sword" (Edward Bulwer-Lytton) *pen* is a stand-in for "the written word."

Motif. A recurring theme, pattern, or symbol.

Narrative hook. An event, action, or detail at the beginning of a story that hooks readers' attention so that they keep reading.

Nonlinear storytelling. The events of the story occur out of chronological order or offer multiple outcomes, as with choose-your-own-adventure stories and video games.

Onomatopoeia. When spoken, a word sounds like what it means: *cackle.*

Overstatement. Closely related to hyperbole, overstatement is exaggeration, often used to emphasize an idea.

Oxymoron. Two words that are essentially opposites and not expected to be used together, often an adjective–noun or adverb–verb combination: *hot ice.*

Paradox. A conflict in concept, reason, or logic. The most famous is the grandfather paradox in the theory of time travel, which asks whether you would cease to exist if you went back in time and caused your own grandfather's death.

Parody. Ridicule or teasing through imitation. Parody can be critical or tributary.

Pastiche. Literary mimicry or imitation of another author or work, usually in tribute or as a form of flattery.

Pathetic fallacy. A type of personification wherein human traits, especially emotions, are attributed to inanimate objects. "Angry skies" would be an example of a pathetic fallacy. Pathetic fallacy was originally coined as an attack on sentimentality in poetry.

Pathos. One of the three modes of persuasion, pathos is an emotional appeal.

Personification. Ascribing human qualities to nonhuman objects and animals.

Plot twist. A surprising or unexpected change in the direction of a story's events.

Plot voucher (or plot coupon). Related to Chekhov's gun, a plot voucher is a promise that a story makes to its audience, often in the form of a mystery or question that will be answered or a character or object that will become important later.

Poetic justice. Good deeds are rewarded or evil actions are punished.

Point-of-view characters (or viewpoint characters). Characters who are in focus throughout a story. George R. R. Martin's *A Song of Ice and Fire* series is written in third-person limited, but each chapter focuses on a different viewpoint character.

Polyptoton. Using two words derived from the same root word in a single sentence. An example would be using *liberate* and *libertine* in the same sentence; both words are formed from the root *liber*, which means "free."

Polysyndeton. Use of multiple conjunctions in close proximity and rapid succession in a single sentence: *we went to the bank and the store and the gas station and the library.*

Predestination paradox. A time-travel paradox in which time travel cannot be used to change the events of the past due to predestination. Also called a causal loop, it establishes a time loop in which certain events and outcomes remain unchanged.

Quibble. Use of an argument, wherein the strictest interpretation of an idea is used as opposed to the original intent.

Red herring. A misleading clue that throws characters (and readers) off the trail of clues that leads to the correct answer or suspect. It is most often used in mysteries when a false suspect is presented as a likely culprit.

Retcon. New information causes past events of a story to be reframed, reinterpreted, or eliminated.

Reveal. A mystery or question is answered or a secret is revealed.

Reversal. A dramatic and polar change happens to the characters or the direction of events in a story, often unexpectedly.

Satire. Criticism through humor, often using irony and overstatement. Jonathan Swift's famous essay "A Modest Proposal" criticized the British treatment of the Irish by suggesting they cook and eat Irish infants, essentially saying, "We treat them so poorly now, we might as well eat their babies."

Self-fulfilling prophecy. A plot device wherein a prophecy is fulfilled due to the actions of characters who knew about the prophecy and were, in many cases, trying to prevent (or cause) it.

Sensory detail. Language that appeals to any or all of the five senses: sight, sound, smell, taste, or touch.

Story arcs. Story arcs occur in episodic storytelling—through several episodes of a television show or several issues of a comic book, for example. In a book series, an arc might stretch across multiple books in the series. Story arcs can occur across any number of installments, including chapters and scenes.

Stream of consciousness. A narrative device or writing style in which thoughts and feelings are presented in a free-flowing and sometimes abstract manner. This style of writing often reflects a sense of thoughts and feelings as opposed to articulated ideas.

Symbolism. A symbol is something that represents something else and is used to enhance a theme, evoke emotion, or establish mood in a narrative.

Synecdoche. A type of metaphor and a subclass of

metonymy in which a term that refers to one element of a thing is used to refer to the whole thing or vice versa. Synecdoche is often used for personification. An example of synecdoche is referring to businesspeople as *suits* or to a car as *wheels*.

Tense (narrative time). Determines whether the story takes place in the past, present, or future.

Thematic patterning. The distribution of theme and motif throughout a story.

Ticking clock scenario. Characters are working against a hard deadline, best exemplified by a bomb set to go off with a timer; the characters only have a limited amount of time to defuse it.

Time jump. A story jumps though time. This could be a forward leap in the narrative ("Ten years later…") or it can occur with flashbacks and flash-forwards.

Time lapse. The narrative uses exposition to quickly cover what has happened in a span of time. Time lapses are used when a story needs to move through time quickly while letting the reader know what's happened during the lapse.

Trope. The classic definition of trope is a figure of speech or the use of figurative language. Recently, trope has come to refer to a convention or common motif, often seen in a particular genre of storytelling. For example, danger in the woods is a common trope in fairy tales.

Understatement. To diminish the importance or significance of something.

Unreliable narrator. A story's narrator lacks credibility and cannot be trusted to provide accurate information about the plot and characters.

Works Cited

Books

The Associated Press Stylebook. New York: Basic Books, 2016.

Baum, Frank L. *The Wonderful Wizard of Oz*. New York: Signet Classics, 1984.

Booker, Christopher. *The Seven Basic Plots: Why We Tell Stories*. New York: Continuum, 2004.

Bradbury, Ray. *Fahrenheit 451*. New York: Simon & Schuster, 2013.

Campbell, Joseph. *The Hero with a Thousand Faces*. Princeton, NJ: Princeton University Press, 1973.

The Chicago Manual of Style. 16th ed. Chicago: University of Chicago Press, 2010.

Collins, Suzanne. *The Hunger Games (Trilogy)*. New York: Scholastic Press, 2008–2010.

Connelly, Michael. Harry Bosh (Series). New York: Little, Brown, 1992–2015.

Conrad, Joseph. *Heart of Darkness*. New York: Global Classics, 1899.

Crichton, Michael, *Jurassic Park*. New York: Knopf, 1990.

Golding, William. *Lord of the Flies*. New York: Penguin Group, 2006.

Herbert, Frank. *Dune*. New York: Berkley Publishing Group, 1977.

Larsson, Stieg. *The Girl with the Dragon Tattoo*. New

York: Random House, 2008.

Lee, Harper. *To Kill a Mockingbird.* New York: HarperCollins, 1985.

Martin, George R. R. *A Song of Ice and Fire (Series).* New York: Bantam Books, 1991–2011.

The Merriam-Webster Dictionary. New ed. Springfield, MA: Merriam-Webster, 2016.

McCarthy, Cormac. *The Road.* New York: Knopf, 2006.

McInerney, Jay. *Bright Lights, Big City.* New York: Random House, 1984.

Orwell, George. *1984.* London: Secker & Warburg, 1949.

Oxford Dictionary of English. 3rd ed. Oxford: Oxford University Press, 2010.

Rowling, J. K. *Harry Potter (Series).* New York: Scholastic, 1998–2007.

Salinger, J. D. *The Catcher in the Rye.* New York: Little, Brown, 1951.

Shakespeare, William. *Romeo and Juliet.* New York: Washington Square Press, 1992.

Swift, Jonathan. "A Modest Proposal." In *A Modest Proposal and Other Satirical Works.* Mineola, NY: Dover, 1996.

Takami, Koushun. *Battle Royale.* San Francisco: Viz Media, 2003.

Tolkien, J. R. R. *Lord of the Rings (Trilogy).* New York: Ballantine Books, 1975.

Tolstoy, Leo. *Strider: The Story of a Horse.* Madison, WI: Borderland Books, 2015.

Vogler, Christopher. *The Writer's Journey: Mythic Structure for Writers*. 3rd ed. Studio City, CA: Michael Wiese Productions, 1998.

Film

Avatar. Directed by James Cameron. 20th Century Fox, 2009.

Batman Begins. Directed by Christopher Nolan. Warner Bros., 2005.

The Breakfast Club. Directed by John Hughes. Universal Pictures, 1985.

Cinderella. Produced by Walt Disney. Walt Disney Productions, 1950.

The Matrix. Directed by the Wachowski Brothers. Warner Bros., 1999.

Star Wars: Episode IV: A New Hope. Directed by George Lucas. 20th Century Fox, 1977.

Sudden Impact. Directed by Clint Eastwood. Warner Bros., 1983.

The Terminator. Directed by James Cameron. Orion Pictures, 1984.

Titanic. Directed by James Cameron. 20th Century Fox, 1997.

When Harry Met Sally. Directed by Rob Reiner. Columbia Pictures, 1989.

The Wizard of Oz. Directed by Victor Fleming. Metro-Goldwyn-Mayer, 1939.

Television

Battlestar Galactica. Television series created by Glen A. Larson. Sci-Fi, 2004–2009.

Friends. Television series created by David Crane and Marta Kauffman. NBC, 1994-2004.

Lost. Television series created by Jeffrey Lieber, J. J. Abrams, and Damon Linedelof. ABC, 2004–2010.

Sex and the City. Television series created by Darren Star. HBO, 1998–2004.

Star Trek (The Original Series). Television series created by Gene Roddenberry. NBC, 1966–1969.

About the Author

Melissa Donovan is the founder and editor of *Writing Forward*, a blog packed with creative writing tips and ideas.

Melissa started writing poetry and song lyrics at age thirteen. Shortly thereafter, she began keeping a journal. She attended Sonoma State University, earning a BA in English with a concentration in creative writing. Since then, Melissa has worked as a copywriter, editor, professional blogger, writing coach, and author.

Writing Forward

Writing Forward features creative writing tips, ideas, tools, and techniques, as well as writing exercises and prompts that offer inspiration and help build skills.

To get more writing tips and ideas and to receive notifications when new books on the craft of writing are released, visit *Writing Forward*.

www.writingforward.com

Adventures in Writing

Adventures in Writing: The Complete Collection takes you on a fun and exciting adventure through the world of creative writing. This volume includes all three books in the Adventures in Writing series with built-in savings:

- *101 Creative Writing Exercises*
- *10 Core Practices for Better Writing*
- *1200 Creative Writing Prompts*

This series is designed to help you on your journey toward becoming a more prolific and skilled writer and to make that journey fun, interesting, and challenging.

Ideal for new and experienced writers alike and perfect for creative writing classes and workshops, *Adventures in Writing: The Complete Collection* will enlighten, inspire, and motivate you with fresh ideas and proven writing techniques.